D0261849

www.southdublinlibraries.ie

South Dublin Libraries

NOTES FROM A LOST TRIBE

Declan Lynch began his writing career at the age of seventeen with Ireland's rock and roll magazine *Hot Press* and now writes for the *Sunday Independent*. He is the author of several works of fiction and non-fiction, including the acclaimed novels *The Rooms* and *The Ponzi Man*, and *Tony 10: The astonishing story of the postman who gambled €10,000,000 . . . and lost it all.*

Arthur Mathews also worked at *Hot Press* and, after a spell in The Joshua Trio, began writing for television. Among the shows he has created and/or written are *Father Ted* (with Graham Linehan), *Toast Of London*, *The Fast Show*, *Black Books* and the film *Wide Open Spaces*.

Among his publications are bogus memoir *Well Remembered Days*, along with *The Book Of Poor Ould Fellas* (with Declan Lynch), *Angry Baby*, and *Toast On Toast*. In the theatre, he created and co-wrote the long running *I, Keano.*

NOTES FROM A LOST TRIBE

The Poor Ould Fellas

DECLAN LYNCH
WITH ARTHUR MATHEWS

HACHETTE
BOOKS
IRELAND

Copyright © 2018
Declan Lynch & Arthur Mathews

First published in 2018 by Hachette Books Ireland

The right of Declan Lynch & Arthur Mathews to be identified as the Authors of the Work has been asserted by them in accordance with the Copyright, Designs and Patents Act 1988.

2

All rights reserved. No part of this publication may be reproduced, stored in a retrieval system, or transmitted, in any form or by any means without the prior written permission of the publisher, nor be otherwise circulated in any form of binding or cover other than that in which it is published and without a similar condition being imposed on the subsequent purchaser.

Cataloguing in Publication Data is available from the British Library

ISBN 978 1 47368 730 1

Typeset in Baskerville by redrattledesign.com

Cover design by Anú Design, Tara, interior design by redrattledesign.com
Printed and bound by Clays Ltd, Elcograf S.p.A.
Inside illustrations: Arthur Mathews

Hachette Books Ireland policy is to use papers that are natural, renewable and recyclable products and made from wood grown in sustainable forests. The logging and manufacturing processes are expected to conform to the environmental regulations of the country of origin.

Hachette Books Ireland
8 Castlecourt Centre
Castleknock
Dublin 15, Ireland

A division of Hachette UK Ltd
Carmelite House, 50 Victoria Embankment, EC4Y 0DZ

www.hachettebooksireland.ie

Contents

Introduction

It has been ten years since *The Book of Poor Ould Fellas* shone a light on one of the darkest corners in one of the darkest rooms in one of the darkest houses in one of the darkest places of Ireland, that which is inhabited by members of the forgotten tribe named in the title.

Cast out from their beloved cosy bars by the smoking ban, further confined to their unhappy dwelling places by the drink-driving laws – 'oh why can't they just have a cup of tea in the pub?' is the cry from the bourgeoisie – tormented by the incessant cooking of TV chefs, they had been effectively abandoned by a society which cares nothing for their modest needs.

With their distinctive dress and their ancient customs, they were surely entitled to be officially designated an ethnic minority by the United Nations, and yet alone among all minorities of any kind they were unrecognised in any meaningful sense, except by the authors of *The Book* about their plight.

And now a decade has passed, and if anything that plight of theirs has become even more desperate. *The*

Book was published just before the Great Crash, which threw up its horrors even for those who were already poor and had no voice despite the rise of social media – the poor ould fellas don't 'do' social media.

Naturally when all the money was being stolen by Wall Street, anything belonging to the poor ould fellas was stolen first – maybe a lump sum in compensation for some hideous entanglement with farm machinery from which they received about two grand after the local solicitor had stolen a share of it.

As regards the internet, they might have found the invention of online gambling to be to their advantage, as betting offices are not suitable for them any more, except they can't open an online account because they tend not to have credit cards. Or laptops. And their enjoyment of sport in general has been diminished by the corporate culture that results in scandals such as the sell-out by the GAA to Sky Sports.

There are many other changes to the social fabric of Ireland that have left the poor ould fellas floundering even more than they had been, if that were possible. In their isolation, they tend to be taken by surprise by certain developments, so that they may arrive at the wedding of their grand-niece, only to discover that she seems to be getting married to a woman. While it makes no difference to them if that is what she wants, it all just adds to their sense of vast befuddlement at the state of the world.

They may not be aware that LGBTQI stands for 'lesbian, gay, bisexual, transgender, queer or questioning and intersex', though they would identify with the sufferings of any oppressed people. Indeed they may qualify under some new heading of their own, since their very existence, let alone their sexuality, is happily dismissed by those who are more fortunate – which is everyone. So it should be LGBTQI And Whatever The Poor Ould Fellas Are, and there must be a campaign for that to be established.

They are also forced to deal with the phenomenon of global warming, with vast windmills being built beside their houses, because nobody cares if they are disturbed by such things. And they receive visits from clever fellows from Dublin, describing the manifold benefits of converting their homes to solar heating – as if this is for their own good, and not the good of the clever fellow from Dublin.

The fact that Ireland is now a multiracial society is also a big change for these men who probably never encountered anyone from any other country until they were about sixty-seven years old (it goes without saying that they have never visited another country). But they are very supportive of the citizenship ceremonies that they see reported on the News, and are wondering if the day will come when they too will be recognised in some meaningful way as citizens of Ireland – up until now, they have merely been perceived as some sort of low-level public nuisance.

They do receive the occasional visit from some despairing social worker, trying to educate them about the benefits of the internet or encouraging them to acquire a smartphone, so that they can sit there and wait for someone to call . . . and wait . . . and wait . . .

Words That Mean Absolutely Nothing to a Poor Ould Fella

Spotify
Streaming
WhatsApp
Hashtag
Transgender toilets
SoundCloud
Transphobic
Woke
Download
Bitcoin
Intersex
Fibre optic
Binary
Non-binary
Falafel
Hotspot
Pesto
LOL
LMAO

Pop-up shop
Hipster
Wi-Fi
Mixed martial arts
Hedge fund
iTunes
Banksy
Smoothie
Snapchat
Othered (though they are the most othered people in the world)

The old six penny piece with the greyhound looked nice

POLITICS AND SOCIETY

LGBTQI and Whatever
the Poor Ould Fellas Are

There was much rejoicing all over Ireland when
the same-sex marriage came in. And it was not just
members of the LGBTQI community who were
celebrating the result of the 2015 referendum to
extend civil marriage rights to same-sex couples.

All decent people were in favour of it, and when a
majority of 62 per cent to 38 per cent was declared,
the sense of achievement was perhaps best expressed
by the author Sebastian Barry, who suggested that
the Yes vote might serve in some small way as an
apology to gay people, for what they had endured
in Ireland during all the lost years of oppression and
discrimination and general unpleasantness.

And now that we're finding ways to apologise to
various minorities who have been scorned or abused
or just ignored, would it be totally out of the question
for Ireland to find some way to say sorry to a certain
section of the community to which such a gesture is
probably long overdue?

Indeed, not only have the poor ould fellas been

oppressed in many ways, they also have the moral authority which derives from the fact that they have never been the oppressor.

They are harmless poor divils in the most literal sense, in that they are almost incapable on any level of inflicting harm on their fellow creatures, man or beast. They are morally and emotionally incapable of it, they are physically incapable of it. They are even legally incapable of it because if a poor ould fella wakes up at dead of night from his fitful sleep to find that his isolated home is being burgled and he happens to have some form of primitive firearm at his disposal, in all likelihood if he discharges that firearm in any way that disturbs the intruders it is he and not them who will be in front of the judge.

As for devices such as Tasers or pepper spray, while they may work quite well when they are used by highly trained police officers in TV crime dramas set in Los Angeles, they are less effective in the trembling hands of a poor ould fella in a remote part of County Longford, transfixed with terror as he faces a gang of bastards from Dublin who are roaring at him to give them things that he hasn't got.

So in such a situation, what the law requires him to do is allow the raiders to beat him savagely with

Things You Will Never, Ever Find the Poor Ould Fellas Doing

Texting

Sexting

Taking a selfie

Composing a tweet

Going away for the weekend

Checking their emails

Going on a Ballymaloe course

Having a romantic night in with a member
  of their own or any other gender

Subscribing to Netflix

Friending someone on Facebook

Going for a run

Reading the paper online

Entering a *Late Late Show* competition

Buying something on eBay

Cycling just for fun

Doing anything just for fun

Drinking a cocktail

Having a stress-busting day in a spa

Entering *MasterChef*
Watching *MasterChef*
Maxing out their credit card
Walking the Camino de Santiago
  de Compostela
Chilling out
Going to the Electric Picnic
Queuing in a bookshop to have the book
  they've just bought signed by the author
Swimming
Buying a copy of *Vanity Fair*
Banking online
Not much banking offline either
Having a few friends around for a barbecue
Growing a beard
Investing in the stock market
Writing a poem
Getting counselling
Listing their hovel
  on Airbnb
Drinking wine
Entertaining
Taking up a hobby
Going to the theatre

They had a woman on the World Cup coverage

baseball bats, or whatever is their weapon of choice, and to shoot his dog, Jack, if Jack offends them in any way. He must also direct them to anything of value he might have in the house, perhaps a small amount of cash that he was hoping against hope would pay for his funeral. He is not technically required to wave them goodbye and wish them 'safe home' as they leave his house and whatever remains of his life in ruins, though he may wish to do so in case his attitude on the night is construed as being needlessly hostile and provocative, and in the hope that they will not come back again next week for another crack at it.

Harmless, harmless poor divils they truly are. Their function on this earth is not to cause harm, but to receive it in every conceivable fashion. So that when some of us see the letters LGBTQI, in the mind's eye we tend to add three more letters – POF.

So we'd be looking at Lesbian, Gay, Bisexual, Transgender, Queer, Intersex and Whatever The Poor Ould Fellas Are, which has a certain ring to it, and which would pay tribute to the poor ould fellas' admirable record down through the years on the whole issue of what used to be called 'gay rights'.

They didn't give a fuck, really, what anyone did to enjoy themselves, they were just generally amazed that anyone living in Ireland could find anything enjoyable to do, of any kind. They were in fact quite liberal-minded, in their utter indifference to how other human beings might choose to define themselves and to conduct their relationships. They really did not care what any other man or woman wanted to call themselves, as long as they didn't call in to them at four in the morning brandishing a sawn-off shotgun.

Indeed such was the extent of their indifference, it was probably as sophisticated in its own way as the attitude of the more progressive citizens of Paris or Copenhagen. If a poor ould fella was walking down the road, and he saw fourteen people of the same sex engaged in some orgiastic activity, he would obviously feel bad about the fact that he might be disturbing them in some way, but otherwise he would have no complaint whatsoever to make, unless to remark that it was perhaps a bit cold for the time of year.

And, in the fullness of time, this marvellous sense of detachment would be evident too in their response to #Repealthe8th, which consisted of a tremendous inability to give one single solitary fuck about all the bad things that the pro-life movement was insisting would happen with a Yes vote.

A poor ould fella does not pass judgement on such

things. If there is any judging to be done, he is not at the front of the queue, he is not even at the back of the queue, he is nowhere to be seen. Though *he* is judged – oh yes he is judged for things such as his conservative attire, for seeing no reason to change the perfectly good suit that he got in a closing-down sale in The Man's Shop in 1957, for not going with the flow of fashion and design and other such ephemera.

So while the POF has not been victimised on account of his sexuality, as such, there is still that argument to be made for adding the POFs to the LGBTQI ticket, on grounds of simple human solidarity. To have them there in a kind of honorary role, as perhaps the only other grouping in the history of Ireland that didn't totally disgrace themselves on this front.

And it would also acknowledge some of the difficulty the same-sex referendum has brought into the lives of the poor ould fellas – difficulty in this case being defined as 'anything that is in any way different to the way they have always done things'.

From County Wexford, for example, we hear of a poor ould fella who received an invitation to the wedding of his grand-niece. A simple enough proposition on the face of it, but not so simple in its execution.

The sight of the postman in the first place actually driving up the long and winding road to the little house was so alarming to the poor ould fella within, it might have been one of those movie scenes in which some woman in rural Iowa whose husband and five sons are off with the US army in the Second World War sees a telegram delivery boy on the horizon – no good can come of it.

So unwanted did this poor ould fella feel in general, he just couldn't conceive of any reason why the postman might be visiting him except to hand him some sort of notice from the government informing him that, unbeknownst to him, he has committed some offence for which he must pay a terrible price.

Nor did he come to the door as the postman shoved

the letter through the box, just in case whatever was being demanded of him had to be collected in person, there and then. So he waited until the delivery van drove away, and then with trembling hands he opened the letter to find it was this invitation to the wedding of his grand-niece, Mary, to Charlie in a few weeks' time in a hotel in Gorey.

This immediately presented him with a terrible dilemma – no, he was not worried that this just didn't give him enough time to get something to wear – he was torn between his natural reluctance to travel fifty miles to such a glittering occasion, probably in a taxi, and the fact that he felt obliged to be there. Forced to be there, if you like, because he is related to this young woman Mary, who somehow hadn't entirely forgotten about his existence – as for his memories of Mary, he thinks he might have bought her a 99 once in Courtown when she was about four years old, but otherwise she would be a total stranger to him.

Then there was the bit about the hotel. This poor ould fella doesn't like hotels, they are too modern, too intimidating in the ways that they expose the limitations of the ancients. He had these visions of being asked to leave by the manager because he is just too old and weak, or being trapped in the door of a hotel lift, forever.

It would have been simpler in a church, where all weddings used to be held, and which is more of a natural habitat for a poor ould fella, a place where he would be able to sit in peace without someone asking him if he wanted a skinny latte for eighteen euro. A place from which he could slip away unnoticed before everyone went to the hotel.

Now with these civil ceremonies, the whole thing happens in the hotel, in this case the Gorey Plaza, and for the poor ould fella there would be no hiding place.

But he decided to go to the wedding anyway, because it was the thing he least wanted to do – instinctively, he felt that was how it was meant to be. The word 'plaza' itself seemed to suggest an environment so alien to him, it might as well have been on Jupiter not in Gorey.

'But that's the way now,' he said to himself, as he shuddered once more at the prospect of a taxi calling for him and him having to say to the driver, 'Take me to the Plaza.' Of course he considered driving his own 1979 Opel Kadett to the event, but he feared that he might draw attention to himself, and perhaps face an interrogation on the side of the road by the gardaí about the NCT, which was only a few years out of date, and the 1997 tax disc and the less-than-perfect overall condition of the vehicle, and so forth.

More Things You Will Never, Ever Find the Poor Ould Fellas Doing

Entering *Operation Transformation*
Watching *Operation Transformation*
Trying out one of the new gins
Trolling
Joining a WhatsApp group
Seeking a grant for a startup
Checking out the new restaurant in town
Having Dermot Bannon around to the hovel
  for *Room to Improve*
Volunteering to go into space
Writing letters to *The Irish Times*
Buying condoms
Exploring the Wild Atlantic Way
Meeting someone for lunch
Going on a diet
Joining the local theatre group or
  musical society
Playing golf
Renewing their passport
Having a red nose or antlers fitted to the
  poor ould car at Christmas

Complaining to the management of a
  service provider
Ordering a pizza to be delivered
Sudoku
Buying a bottle of water, still or sparkling
Picking up a copy of *The Happy Pear:
  Recipes for Happiness*
Setting up surround-sound on the television
Choosing a packet of gluten-free sausages
Buying a book on Amazon
Watching an episode of *Game of Thrones*
Doing a course
Having friends over for the Premier
  League matches on Super Sunday
Going to IKEA
Phoning someone just to catch up
Practising mindfulness
Selecting an amusing ring-tone
Flossing
Playing the guitar
Getting a coffee to
  take away
Doing press-ups
Moving house
Going for a long walk on
  the beach

The nephew said Skyping is cheaper than the phone, but I don't know what it is . . .

And so he found himself on the big day being dropped off at the Plaza by a taxi driver with a Dublin accent – he had never known any other kind – who charged him €300 but said he would take him back home that evening for a special discount rate of an extra €250. The poor ould fella didn't have that kind of money on him, but in a welter of embarrassment he said that he had the money at home in an old biscuit tin. This should be acceptable to the taxi driver, which at least guaranteed that he would actually leave the poor ould fella home, as arranged.

In the room where the civil ceremony was taking place, about a hundred guests waited in a state of great anticipation, none of them acknowledging the poor ould fella as he slipped into the back row, none of them having a clue who he was or what he was doing there. Likewise he recognised none of them, because he can't see very well.

He did notice however that Charlie, the groom, was not waiting at the front of the room, which he felt was unusual. But, then again, maybe they don't do that any more either, maybe bride and groom just arrive at the same time.

Then he was sure that his eyesight must be going entirely, because the next thing he sees is the bride and the bridesmaid – he can't quite make out which of them is Mary, and probably couldn't even with 20/20

vision – walking past him, at which point he assumed that the bould Charlie must indeed be somewhere at the top of the room, waiting for Mary. The poor ould fella just can't see him, but he surely must be there.

And so this strange event proceeded, with the poor ould fella trying to follow the unfamiliar ceremony, becoming increasingly puzzled by various remarks whispered by the guests sitting near him. 'Isn't Charlie looking absolutely beautiful?', made very little sense to him, for example, but he let it go anyway, assuming that he must have misheard, that they must be talking about Mary, not Charlie, that somehow it is he who is in the wrong.

'I think they went to the same dressmaker', was another line that he overheard, another curveball.

Slowly, it was starting to dawn on him – Mary was getting married to a woman.

Until now he had associated the name Charlie mainly

with Charlie Haughey. And while he accepted that women could call themselves anything they wanted these days, and could get married to anyone they wanted, still his many years of conditioning had led him to assume that this would be a more old-fashioned arrangement.

Ultimately, of course, he didn't give a fuck one way or the other, but it certainly contributed to his feelings of confusion on the day, to find that he was a guest at a lesbian wedding without realising it.

Later, in the taxi on the way home, the driver engaged in asinine banter during which he shared his idiotic views on same-sex marriage (he was of course against it), informing the poor ould fella of the case whereby two old men who are not gay, but who are very good friends, were planning to get married so that one of them could leave everything to the other without having to pay tax on the inheritance.

By now the poor ould fella was just not equipped to process such information, and still, at the end of a long and bewildering day, the most surprising thing was yet to come.

As he took the last few quid out of the biscuit tin to pay the fare, he was fully expecting the taxi man to pounce on him and force him to cough up any other valuables he might have, and then perhaps kill him for a bit of amusement.

Instead the driver just took the money, and laughed.

Bullshit

Cyclists all dressed up in cycling gear
People carrying bottles of water around
  with them
Fair City
GAA goalkeepers running up the field
  to take free kicks
Chiropractors
NAMA
Street theatre
The RTÉ Player (whatever that is)
Brexit
Showering every day
Showering in general
The Cork Examiner
  becoming *The Examiner*
Self-help books
Global warming

When we were young, we were told just to get on with it.

The Free Travel

Since the day it was invented by Charlie Haughey, there had never been a bad word said about the Free Travel Scheme – how could there be?

It was one of the three good things that Haughey did in his entire career, as against the three thousand bad things he did, but it was such a remarkably good thing, it almost cancelled out all the other stuff. Almost.

Still, the fact that at least half of its beneficiaries were poor ould fellas made it somewhat unique in Irish political history. And no doubt Haughey eventually came to think of it as some sort of an aberration, unable to understand how he alone had had the right instincts, and vowing never to make such a mistake again.

He did it though, and it has stood as one of his monuments, along with the Artists' Tax Exemption and . . . eh . . . whatever the other one was.

Indeed the artists' exemption has become devalued over time, as it was originally intended to save various impoverished poets and painters and other such bohemian types from dying of actual starvation, though it immediately became quite popular with the writers of airport thrillers who would move to a mansion in Wicklow to avoid paying tax in England. And it would later bring many rock stars to Ireland for the same purpose, while the destitute poets and painters continued to struggle. Certainly, they would be paying no tax on their income, it's just they had no income anyway.

So maybe that is how Haughey envisaged it, a kind of a black joke on poor artistic types, which had unintended consequences. The Free Travel too would develop in ways that he hadn't quite foreseen, but in its essence it remained an unimpeachably good thing, an unambiguous benefit conferred at least in part on the poor ould fellas.

Nor was Haughey just trying to buy their votes here – well, he was always doing that up to a point – but in general he didn't need to buy the votes of the poor ould fellas because they tended to vote for him and his party anyway. Having realised over a long period of time that Ireland was utterly, irredeemably corrupt, they felt it made some sort of sense to vote for the most obviously corrupt leader, there was a kind of a philosophical consistency to it. And they knew it made no difference anyway, regardless of who was elected they would always be screwed.

Except on this one occasion, when somehow, inexplicably, they were told that from now on, they would be entitled to travel on public transport in Ireland for free. Just that.

They searched long and hard for a catch, knowing how much the government enjoys annoying them and frustrating them and thwarting them when it isn't completely ignoring them, but with this there really was no trick. In order to get the bus from Offaly to Mayo they didn't have to first go to Waterford or something of that nature. In order to get the train from Westport to Athlone they didn't have to stand on the platform reciting a poem in French or do anything at all really, just show up at the appointed hour and take that train.

Not that they had much interest in that side of it, as such. The poor ould fellas would rarely get the urge to make such journeys as they were perfectly capable of not enjoying themselves in their own homes, rather than not enjoying themselves on the public transport networks of Ireland. So it really was the thought that counted – just the thought that, in theory at least, they were permitted to do this thing that many other people were not permitted to do, that for once there was some form of discrimination in their favour rather than against them.

Indeed at times they would just become bamboozled by it all, and some of them would spend hours trying to understand it, trying to find the catch that they were sure must be there somewhere, their poor ould heads weary from the effort as if they had been presented with one of those mathematical tests that featured in the film *A Beautiful Mind*, which none of them ever saw.

Try as they might, they could see nothing wrong with it, nor indeed could anyone else. Wherever you rambled in the towns and counties of Ireland you'd hear many things, but not until some time in late 2016 or thereabouts would you hear a bad word about the Free Travel.

No, you would hear only good things.

Indeed at times you could form the impression that the Free Travel was viewed with such affection by the people, it was the only reason some of them were bothering to stay alive at all. That the scheme had found its way so deeply into our consciousness, it had become the very definition of getting old in Ireland.

Anyone in the vicinity of sixty-six would tend to say, 'I'm getting the bus pass,' rather than describing themselves as 'pensioners' or 'retirees' – anyone, that is, apart from the poor ould fellas, because if you're one of them it doesn't matter what you say, nobody is listening anyway.

But they are thinking about you, those clever people who run the country, and if they suspect even for a moment that there might be something that brings some solace, however insignificant, into your otherwise meaningless existence, it seems they will make it their business to take it away from you, to 'discontinue' it, as they say.

Perhaps it was this impulse which was driving these suggestions that were now being heard for the first time, that the Free Travel may have to be 'reviewed', or modified in some way, perhaps by imposing an annual charge of 50 euro – the hope would be that poor ould fellas and other elderly types would not

have the wherewithal to renew their subscription, and thus would not be troubling our already overburdened transport system with their journeys to the hospital to be informed by an equally overburdened medic that they have three weeks to live and, by the way, it won't be pleasant.

Yes, that would tidy up the books somewhat for those clever people who are forever wondering if there is anything – anything at all – that gives the poor ould fellas some pleasure, however meagre and however dubious, so they can cut it or curtail it or otherwise take the good out of it.

No doubt they'd had their eye on this one for a long time, allegedly because the numbers of people eligible for it have been rising, probably beyond that which was originally envisaged by Charlie Haughey when he ran it up the flagpole, and a grateful nation saluted.

Now those clever people in their clever, clever way were putting it out there that the scheme is being so overused, a case could be made to an increasingly mature people, putting forward a measured economic argument in favour of some, shall we say . . . adjustments.

So out of nowhere, it seemed, we were hearing these voices trying to talk a bit of sense into us, telling us that we will have to get real about this Free Travel lark. And their numbers sounded quite impressive – they said that one-quarter of the population is now entitled to the Free Travel – and yet somehow unimpressive.

You don't have to be John Maynard Keynes to see that if the elderly and the infirm and their spouses or carers had to pay for all these free trips from, say, Athlone to Galway and back again, many of them wouldn't go at all or wouldn't even think of going. So we'd be losing a mental-health dividend right there. Nor would they be contributing to the economies of Athlone or Galway as they are doing now, perhaps buying a cup of tea or a bowl of oxtail soup or even the occasional glass of stout in a friendly bar, which would be accompanied by a relaxing cigarette if that small pleasure hadn't also been taken away from them.

And unlike child benefit, which is given to very rich people, we can probably take it for granted that no rich old person will be taking that free bus ride from Arklow to Enniscorthy just because they can.

But when we look beyond the numbers, we can see this as perhaps the perfect example of how the prevailing orthodoxies of our time have become estranged from any considerations of ordinary human happiness, in particular the happiness of a certain breed of elderly gentleman.

The Free Travel, which like the Artists' Exemption is actually something we can call our own, had become so beloved over time, so cherished in the hearts of the people, you could nearly call it our equivalent of the American Dream.

If the American Dream says that if you work hard in that great land of endless possibility, you can create a kind of personalised vision of paradise, then the Irish Dream goes something like this: if you work hard, in this country which keeps going down the tubes for everyone but the insiders, which seems to have no coherent philosophy of government except the desire to support those more fortunate than ourselves, at the end of all that work you have virtually nothing, and even less to look forward to, except this – that some fine day, even if you have no money, you can get a bus from Drogheda to Castlebellingham just because you feel like it, just because it's there.

It's not exactly a crazy dream, it may not even be a very beautiful dream, but all things considered, it has been the Irish Dream.

It has been the dream of the poor ould fellas, the only one that has not been shattered by the ruling classes.

But they're working on it, by Christ, they're working on it.

Even More Things You Will Never, Ever Find the Poor Ould Fellas Doing

Having muesli for breakfast
Wearing headphones
Doing a twelve-step programme
Sunbathing
Enjoying a bit of banter
Smoking cannabis
Changing around the furniture
Spending an evening at a bowling alley
Eating a Magnum
Making jam
Drinking herbal tea
Shopping around for a
 better phone deal
Yoga
Playing Scrabble
Going to a rugby match
Trying out a few craft
 beers
Wearing novelty
 socks

Sheila got rid of the curtains, and got some blinds put in

The Zero Tolerance

In our work on behalf of the Poor Ould Fellas, one of the more contentious areas is the issue of them driving home from the pubs with perhaps a few drops of alcohol on board, technically above the legal limit. Yes, we get some blowback on that, blowback in this case meaning the sort of criticism that seems vaguely reasonable on a superficial level, yet that somehow takes very little account of the true nature of the human condition and of life on earth in general.

In the mind's eye, for example, what sort of person do we see when we think about the dangerously drunk driver? Would the first image that comes to us be that of an elderly man driving a very old car very slowly along a road that has had almost no other traffic on it since about 1956? We do not think so.

Indeed, in the mind's eye we are seeing something that is a tad different to that unthreatening vista. We are seeing someone much younger, in a much newer and much faster car. We are seeing people who have had far more to drink than any poor ould fella could even contemplate at this stage of his life, cruising along the superhighway. Indeed we are hardly seeing the poor ould fella at all, but we are seeing quite a few rich young fellas.

And while a zero-tolerance approach in this domain of road safety has its merits, we feel it is a shame that zero tolerance is not the watchword in other areas too – we would like to see zero tolerance of the systematic destruction of the entire way of life of the indigenous people whose cause we are representing here. We would like to see zero tolerance of the casual disregard for the few small things that keep them going, zero tolerance for the many ways in which they are excluded from life's feast.

But we do not see zero tolerance of these things, indeed we see . . . whatever the opposite of zero tolerance is.

And so we find ourselves in the company of strange bedfellows here, we find that there are times when we are saying things that the famed Kerry TD Michael Healy-Rae might say, things that the other famed Kerry TD Danny Healy-Rae might say, even things that their father the late Kerry TD Jackie Healy-Rae might have said.

Because one of the odd things about this issue of

drinking and driving is that it is those who identify themselves as peasants, not the bourgeoisie, who seem to have a sense of the philosophical dimension. Not that they are aware of this in an abstract sense – they are, after all, peasants – yet their raw instincts on this are quite deceptively nuanced.

In their bucolic way, they see that no human endeavour of any kind is entirely free from danger. And that if we measured everything we do solely in terms of its safety, we would end up doing virtually nothing – which by an odd coincidence is where the poor ould fellas increasingly find themselves, prohibited as they are from driving home after a night in the old tavern that they can't enjoy any more anyway, unless they want also to enjoy the double pneumonia they will get from standing outside in the cold to have a smoke.

Of course it is assumed by the modern lads that the poor ould fellas are great fans all round of the Healy-Raes, but then many things that are assumed by the modern lads are not necessarily the case. Certainly the Healy-Raes can give the impression that they are not just on the side of

the poor ould fellas, but are themselves members of that tribe. And yet in one very important respect they are not poor ould fellas at all – it's the 'poor' bit we're talking about here. Because they are not poor, they are rich. There is a difference.

There is a very big difference there, in truth. But in other matters pertaining to their less-well-off brethren, the Healy-Raes would have a certain insight into these issues as for many years they have been running a public house in Kilgarvan, County Kerry, the success of which owes much to the patronage of a certain sort of clientele who are, shall we say, of limited means, of advanced years, and of the male gender. Perhaps in honour of this, the most prominent of the Healy-Raes, the one called Michael, routinely dons the cap and the rest of the traditional costume of that clientele – indeed as a matter of principle he will never take the cap off, even in a television studio, which may seem somewhat strange to various foreign sophisticates over here on a visit, and even to our own alleged sophisticates if truth be told. But it is his look, his brand, his statement, and it shows solidarity with an all-but-extinct species of a kind that we do not see from the self-styled 'modernisers'. There are even times when the man with the cap seems to be ahead of these essentially bourgeois elements in his enunciation of some of the core principles of existence.

Unlike the bourgeoisie, the Healy-Raes are not satisfied simply to state that anything that may contribute in any way to the avoidance of accidents is self-evidently good. Because to them, there are other things that are also self-evidently good. And in their awareness of the complexity of human existence, and perhaps for reasons which must remain mysterious even to themselves, they feel obliged to draw attention to some of these things.

Things like the quality of life of the poor ould fellas, who in an ideal world of Danny Healy-Rae's making, would be issued with some kind of special permit that would allow them to have 'two or three glasses of Guinness' and then drive home in a vehicle which probably can't go faster than 20 miles an hour anyway on a lonely country road, so lonely that there would be nobody around for them to kill.

And it would be quite a novelty too for the poor ould fellas to be given something – anything – that they want, anything that might make their proverbial journey to the grave just a little bit easier.

After all, they can hardly be walking home the few miles, as their movements are not that fluid any more. Indeed, if you are walking behind a poor ould fella in the street, and you call his name, he will move his upper body around in such a mechanical fashion, it looks like he's performing a kind of a three-point turn. Or even a five-point turn, on the cold mornings. Indeed by the time he has manoeuvred himself around to face you, the chances are you will already be striding twenty yards ahead of him, and calling back to him, which now requires him to do the three-point turn in the other direction.So it would be no harm in the slightest to allow these men a few of the small concessions that they require, on or off the roads.

They can't have a cigarette with their glass of stout any more and soon they may not even be able to have the glass of stout, if they want to get home in their preferred vehicle. And this will reduce their lifestyle to a level of

nothingness that makes the more minimalist work of Beckett seem like the definitive Broadway production of *Hello, Dolly!*.

So they remain the only minority in this country whose ancient ways can be utterly disrespected, regardless of the damage that this is doing to their quality of life and to their health – in particular to their mental health which is at its most precarious when they do not have a glass of stout in front of them in a cosy bar – and instead are waiting fearfully in their homes for something really bad to happen.

Then we will hear a panel on *The Marian Finucane Show* speaking piously about 'rural isolation', making no connection between this and the proposed abolition of the only recreation that makes the existence of the rurally isolated even vaguely tolerable.

Intuitively, even the haute bourgeoisie know in their souls who are likely to cause road accidents. They know that the most dangerous thing happening on the roads these days is the use of mobile phones, and that the poor ould fellas are perhaps the least likely of all motorists to be distracted from their driving becasue they are on their smartphones.

No, they will not be taking their eyes off the road to compose a reply to a text from some other poor ould fella. They will not even be sending a quick LOL or IMAO followed by a string of kisses. Nor will they be Instagramming or putting the final touches to a Snapchat story as they drive home from that cosy bar which is their only consolation.

We have also heard it said that the Healy-Raes are resorting to low peasant cunning when they complain about overgrown hedges being a cause of accidents, due to restrictions on hedge-cutting advocated by 'do-gooders' seeking, *inter alia*, to protect certain species of birds. To which one might add that the 'do-gooders' indeed seem more concerned with the survival of the lesserspotted owl than that of the lesserspotted ould fella.

And here they are unwittingly straying into the same territory as the unrepentant peasantry, with this tacit acknowledgment that there are perhaps more things in heaven and on earth than are dreamed of in the absolutist philosophy of the Department of Transport. Because, after all, there may be a few cases in Irish history in which an overgrown hedge has actually contributed in some small way to an accidental death on the roads – in which case it would be consistent with a zero-tolerance approach to cut thcm all down, and to hell with the birds, even if it was to save just one of those human lives.

'What is wrong with a glass of water or a cup of coffee?', the voices of Official Ireland will say, sitting in their lovely RTÉ studio, wondering why the poor ould fellas can't enjoy their weekly visit to the pub without the promise of some alcoholic drink.

Even though these men ask for so little, still they are being blamed for asking for the wrong thing.

Yes, there is a lack of imagination on the part of the peasant publicans who could be developing new strategies in the area of transportation, organising buses or encouraging customers to bring their spouses along as designated drivers, perhaps by giving them cheap minerals.

But alas, our old friend the 'rural isolation' does not lend itself to such seemingly practical solutions: the poor ould fellas might get vexed if they are herded onto a mini-bus with a bunch of other poor ould fellas – they tend to be solitary creatures, which also makes it unlikely that they would have a spouse or that they would admit it if they did.

Yes, they can be a bit 'odd'. Which is not a crime; though, like their last remaining pleasure in life, no doubt it will be soon.

Yet Even More Things You Will Never, Ever Find the Poor Ould Fellas Doing

Voting for a contestant on *Dancing With the Stars*

Making an appointment with a dental hygienist

Putting those blue discs in Tesco into a 'favourite charity' container

Replacing their light bulbs with eco-friendly, energy-saving ones

Going to life-drawing classes

Buying a Blu-ray player

Bingeing on box sets (unless *The Riordans* gets released on a twelve-disc compilation)

They'll have to weigh it at the post office …

The Poor Ould Fella's
IDEAL
TV Schedule

1.00 **THE LATE LATE SHOW REVISITED** – Highlights of old episodes of the Late Late presented by Gay Byrne.

1.30 **ONE MAN AND HIS DOG** – Sheepdog trials.

2.00 **TOM AND JERRY** – More hilarious antics from the cartoon duo.

2.30 **MANNIX** – Another mystery for private investigator Joe Mannix to solve.

3.30 **THE VIRGINIAN** – In a case of mistaken identity, Trampas is pursued by a bounty hunter, while The Virginian gets an unusual request for help. Starring James Drury, with Doug McClure and Clu Gulager.

4.30 **THE RIORDANS** – Nostalgic episode of the Irish farming drama. Tom and Benjy have a falling-out over plans for a new shed.

5.30 **THE BEST OF HALL'S PICTORIAL WEEKLY** – A classic episode of the satirical show, featuring Cha and Miah, the Minister for Hardship, and the latest from Ballymagash.

6.00 **THE ANGELUS** – Just a holy picture and bells, thanks.

6.01 **THE NEWS** – Presented by Eileen Dunne. Weather with Evelyn Cusack.

7.00 **THE GALWAY RACES** – The annual festival kicks off at Ballybrit, with Ted Walsh.

8.30 **NATIONWIDE** – A special episode of the popular magazine programme with Mary Kennedy and Anne Cassin in Galway.

9.00 **THE NEWS** – More news, presented by Eileen Dunne. Weather with Evelyn Cusack.

9.30 **7 DAYS** – From the vaults, a reprise of the current affairs programme presented by David Thornley, John O'Donoghue, and Brian Farrell. Tonight: The Arms Trial.

10.00 **BIG TOM REMEMBERED** – A tribute to the King of Country.

11.15 **LATE NEWS** – Presented by Eileen Dunne. Weather with Evelyn Cusack.

11.20 **CLOSEDOWN**

The Poor Ould Fella's
NIGHTMARE
TV Schedule

1.00 **LOOSE WOMEN** – The lunchtime chat show.

2.00 **JEREMY KYLE** – Shouting and roaring.

3.00 **ROOM TO IMPROVE** (Repeat) Another repeat of the house makeover show with Dermot Bannon.

4.00 **HOME OF THE YEAR** (Repeat) – Another repeat of the show which brings us inside Ireland's most spectacular homes.

4.30 **DR. PHIL** – Talk show with life strategist Dr Phil McGraw.

5.30 **HOME AND AWAY** – The latest from Summer Bay.

6.00 **XPOSE** – The latest from the catwalk.

6.30 **CELEBRITY MASTERCHEF** – How will the stars fare in the restaurant kitchen of a 3-star Michelin chef?

7.30 **TOP GEAR** – The all-action show featuring Jeremy Clarkson.

8.30 **THE RESTAURANT** – An Irish celebrity presents a meal to three judges including Marco Pierre White.

9.00 **BOTCHED** – Plastic surgery gone wrong.

9.30 **THE LATE LATE SHOW** – Presented by Ryan Tubridy.

11.30 **LATE NIGHT MOVIE – DJANGO UNCHAINED** 2012 revisionist Western directed by Quentin Tarantino.

1.30 **NON-STOP PARTY MUSIC** – Top 100 Acid House classics.

The Pilot Schemes

When we started to campaign on behalf of the poor ould fellas, there was an instant and enthusiastic response from readers. In the pages of the *Sunday Independent* and later in the first *Book of Poor Ould Fellas*, we drew attention to a scandalous culture of social exclusion, and found that readers were able to identify with many of the vignettes which we presented.

They would contact us with their own stories of the indignities endured by poor ould fellas who were known to them, but perhaps not well enough known for them to do anything about it – except to tell us in the hope that we would pass it on to other readers. And so it went, so the great wheel turned . . .

Which might have seemed a tad unhelpful, in any real terms were it not for the fact that one of these readers turned out to be the former President of Ireland, Mary McAleese.

That's right – only the president, only the first citizen, only the guardian of the Constitution. Only one of the most influential people in the country, that's all, only one Mary Patricia McAleese.

Though we should add that when we say that she was alerted to the problems of the poor ould fellas as a direct result of reading our work on the subject, we are of course making that up.

We have not the slightest idea what the now former President McAleese would read or would not read, all that we know is this: on the off-chance that she hadn't been reading *The Book of Poor Ould Fellas*, she still somehow found a way to start talking in a highly familiar way about certain individuals in our society who are poor, who are ould and who are fellas.

So we'll just leave that one with you, and we'll put it like this: reports in the Dublin media were suggesting that the president was going to embark on an 'initiative', because she and her husband Martin 'had noticed an absence of older men attending functions to which she had been invited'.

And then there was the GAA – yes, apart from the single most important citizen in the land, the most important organisation in the land had also been reading *The Book of Poor Ould Fellas*, and had been so inspired by it they had embarked on an 'initiative' of their own. Though again we should add in passing that we are absolutely making that up, that we have no way of knowing if we started them on it and that they probably wouldn't tell us even if we did.

So along with the president they took this 'initiative', if 'initiative' here means something on which someone else had already taken the initiative.

Joining forces, these two great powers declared the GAA Social Initiative, which, by one account, was 'the pilot phase of the social scheme which she [the president] sparked to offset the isolation of some of the two hundred thousand men over sixty-five years old who live in this country'.

Now, when they say that she 'sparked' it, perhaps it would be a tad more accurate to say that she didn't spark it, as such, but that it was already sparked and burning wildly due to the fact that we had already sparked it

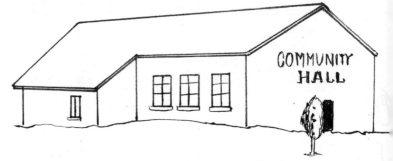

– but, again, this slight distinction would perhaps be attributable not to the former president herself but to the Dublin media.

Anyway, it happened in Croke Park, this launch of the pilot scheme, which was promising in one sense if not quite in another. Yes, the poor ould fellas have a great attachment to anything happening in Croke Park, even if it's only about them, but they've seen a fair few 'pilot schemes' coming and going, when in truth all they are looking for is the sort of 'pilot scheme' which has Philomena Begley on the telly now and again. Philomena and her Ramblin' Men.

Any chance of a pilot scheme for that, no? Any chance of any sort of a scheme, pilot or otherwise, to have a Johnny McEvoy song played on the radio now and again?

The World of Records

Likes:

'White Christmas' – Bing Crosby

'Four Roads to Glenamaddy' – Big Tom

'One Day at a Time' – Gloria

'The Boston Burglar' – Johnny McEvoy

'Bring Flowers of the Rarest' – Canon
  Sydney MacEwan

'Do You Want Your Ould Lobby Washed
  Down?' – Brendan Shine

'House with the Whitewashed Gable'
  – Joe Dolan

'Rhinestone Cowboy' – Glen Campbell

'Nearer My God To Thee' (as sung in the old
  black-and-white film *A
Night to Remember*
  when the *Titanic* is
  going down)

Dislikes:

'Get Lucky' – Daft Punk (played constantly
   in the 'beer garden' outside the pub
   where they are forced to smoke)
'Single Ladies (Put a Ring On It)' –
   Beyoncé (played constantly on the bus on
   the way to the hospital for the operation)
'Simply the Best' – Tina Turner (played
   constantly on the telly
   when anyone does
   anything that is any good)
And all other songs written
   and recorded during the
   past thirty years

Not even President McAleese, working in tandem
with the GAA, could swing that one, apparently, and in
fact they in turn were working in tandem with excellent
bodies such as the Irish Farmers' Association, Senior
Help Line, Third Age, Macra na Feirme, Muintir na
Tíre and the gardaí.

That's a pretty long tandem there, at the end of
which a man could still be listening all day to Radio
Éireann and never hear even a passing mention of the
names Philomena Begley or Johnny McEvoy, and as

for a TV appearance by either of those outstanding artistes, that would also be a no.

But then all these bodies and all the fine ladies and gentlemen on them, working in tandem, had loftier ambitions for the poor ould fellas.

They brought 160 of them to Croke Park for the big launch, the 160 hailing from the four counties in which the scheme was being piloted: Fermanagh, Wexford, Mayo and Kerry. It was said that three of the men from Kerry had never been in Dublin before – as if this was in some way surprising or even a bad thing.

Grand words were spoken, about the need for 'personal contact with older men who live alone and are identified as disengaged from the community to a greater or lesser extent'. Moreover, 'personal invitations' would be issued to 'special social events which will be sports related, friendly, local and welcoming'.

They'd thought of everything really, apart from the seemingly unattainable vision of having a record by Larry Cunningham played on the radio now and again, which is more or less all that the poor ould fellas are asking. One 'Lovely Leitrim' or one 'Slaney Valley' would be as good as a thousand 'special social events' to them.

By all means let them be driven to the GAA social centre and driven back home again after an evening in the company of other poor ould fellas, wondering which one of them is going to die first, or even which of them will last the night, but none of that would be necessary if only there was the odd episode of *The Virginian* or *The High Chaparral* on the telly in the afternoon.

Still, the eternally well-meaning President McAleese went on to host a forum for older men in Áras an Uachtaráin, at which she quoted the former GAA President Dr Mick Loftus who referred to the relevant demographic as 'fellas who never leave their houses'.

There was even an RTÉ news feature around that time that called them 'the fellas who live up the lane'.

Now we're just wondering here . . . we heard all this talk from not one president but two, and from various quarters of the Dublin media, about 'older men who live alone', and 'the fellas who never leave their houses', and 'the fellas who live up the lane', and, like, really, we're just wondering . . . would 'the poor ould fellas' kind of cover most of it? Would those, by any chance, be the words they were looking for?

After all the pilot schemes and the initiatives and even the forum could they not find it within themselves to direct people to the true original source in these matters?

I mean, we wouldn't be making any great claim here if we pointed out that 'the fellas who never leave their houses' and 'the fellas who live up the lane' lack a certain something that 'the poor ould fellas' has – that certain something being that our one is better.

And yet despite this apparent unease with earthy language, with words that are of the very soil that was worked so thanklessly for so long by the poor ould fellas, we must at least acknowledge that Mrs McAleese and the GAA and Muintir na Tíre and their ilk have made some kind of a contribution to the cause – we acknowledge that, and some day maybe they'll even acknowledge us. But then again we know that they won't.

To their credit, we remember that RTÉ news report in which they went up the lane to talk to an ould fella who lives there, and we applauded its dirty realism. On the mantelpiece behind the poor ould fella there were a few In Memoriam cards, which would be typical of the style of home accessorising favoured by these men – they would not have much in the way of Warhol reproductions or moody photographs of Paris by Robert Doisneau or life-affirming drawings by Pauline Bewick on the walls.

No, they would prefer to fill their shelves with these cards, featuring some kind of a holy poem and a small black-and-white photo of the deceased.

Taking the poor ould fellas to the GAA social centre has its merits, in an abstract kind of way, but for the most part their lives are not about making new friends, but burying old ones.

So they do not surround themselves with calming images of the Buddha or with posters that feature inspirational quotes, but with pictures of other poor ould fellas who have gone to a better place. A far, far better place.

The World of Food

Likes:

A chop
The small mixed grill
The medium mixed grill
The large mixed grill
The small Irish breakfast
The medium Irish breakfast
The full Irish breakfast
Irish stew
Soup (oxtail) and sandwich (ham or cheese)
Bacon and cabbage
Steak (well done) and onions
Hamburger and chips
Smoked cod and chips
Batterburger and chips
Sausage and chips
Carvery lunch (as long as it's roast beef)
Tin of beans or peas
Eggs boiled, fried or scrambled
  (not poached)
Custard and stewed apple
Ice-cream (wafers)
Biscuits (fig rolls,
  digestives,
  custard creams,
  rich tea)

Dislikes:
Curry
Spaghetti bolognese
Pizza
Chinese
Lasagne
Kebabs
Moussaka (whatever that is)
Beef stroganoff (whatever that is)
Goulash
Quiche
Chili
Smoked salmon
Prawns
Prawn cocktail
Anything 'organic'
Anything that is advertised
 by Marco Pierre White
And any food of any kind
  that is cooked on
  television

The 'Independent Financial Advisors'

During the boom, the poor ould fellas would be visited in their homes from time to time by various characters calling themselves 'independent financial advisors' and the like, offering their services.

Indeed it is a tribute to the diligence of these 'independent financial advisors' that they were not deterred in any way by the unpleasantness of the task which might face them. There are more squeamish individuals who might baulk at the idea of spending time in the company of poor ould fellas, of entering their homes for any purpose, given the justifiable fears of what might await them there − the spartan living conditions, the drab furnishings and the downbeat décor in general, the strange smells that might be coming from Jack the dog, the dampness, which might be anything really, the old-fashioned toilet arrangements, the offer of tea in a cup, which may fall slightly short of the very highest standards demanded by the health inspectors, along with some sort of a biscuit of dubious provenance . . .

And there would also be the prospect of having to shout very loudly in order to communicate with their prey – er, I mean their client – which could make this an exhausting encounter all round, for what might well be a relatively small reward.

But they were willing to do the hard yards, as they would call it in the rugby-playing schools from which many of them had emerged, wild with desire for other people's money. They would see their dealings with the poor ould fellas as a kind of a test of their manhood, a mark of what they are prepared to endure in order to shake down even the most unfortunate of their victims, er, I mean their customers.

No actually I mean their victims, their prey, with whom they would be sitting down for as long as it took, in order to achieve the desired result – which was of course to relieve them of whatever few shillings they had, in return for nothing but a few lines of bullshit in some meaningless document.

They took pride in it, boasting to one another of the investment 'products' that they managed to sell to the poor ould fellas, many of whom though very near to death, were still agreeing to invest in things that would only start making a return in the year 2046.

'God forbid'. . . these were the pious words that

would stick in the minds of the poor ould fellas as they were being shafted by these smooth-talking dudes in their lovely suits, as well-turned-out as their victims were modestly attired. 'If you should die . . . God forbid', the independent financial advisor would say, trying to interest some eighty-two-year-old man in a pension plan that would come to fruition in thirty years time, but which would pay out a lump sum to Jack the dog, 'If you should die . . . God forbid.'

As the financial advisor opened up his laptop – the first time the poor ould fella had ever seen such a thing – he would start talking about 'the need to diversify your portfolio,' correctly guessing that the 'portfolio' in question at that point in time was under the bed in the next room in a USA Assorted biscuit tin which had been a Christmas gift back in 1969.

When the poor ould fella would confess to the whereabouts of his assets, such as they were, the independent financial advisor would chide him gently, advising him that he must start making his money work for him, meaning, of course, that the poor ould fella must start making his money work for the independent financial advisor – there is a difference, though it was lost on the unfortunate victim, who was now just embarrassed that he had been so foolish as to place his funds anywhere but in the myriad of high-performance financial vehicles that were now being offered to him. For a small fee.

Yes, there would be charges, he was told, in setting up this diverse portfolio, but such were the long-term benefits to be had, he'd barely notice them. Working the laptop, the independent financial advisor would show the poor ould fella a series of highly impressive graphs, showing an upward curve almost to infinity. And because his eyesight was not the best, the poor ould fella would find it hard to deduce from the small print that he would need to live for another hundred and fifty years to start really coining it.

He was also informed, 'in the interests of transparency', that some of his funds would be invested in the stock market, which would naturally make him somewhat nervous, as he had no idea what the stock market is or what it might do with the two grand that he had left in the world.

Here the independent financial advisor would be most reassuring about this strategy whereby the poor ould fella would give all his money to the financial services professionals, so they could 'grow' it – 'It's what I do with my own money', he might say. Or 'take it from me, these guys know what they're doing'.

And indeed these guys *did* know what they were doing. They were taking all the money in all the proverbial biscuit tins in the world and gambling it away for their sport – and getting away with it in the end because that's how it works.

But such macroeconomic visions were beyond the poor ould fellas, as they dutifully brought out the biscuit tin to show to the financial advisor, apologising in advance for any offence that might be caused by such unsophisticated arrangements.

Taking the cash and handing the poor ould fella a bullshit receipt in return, the independent financial advisor would press home his advantage, talking about the 'equity' which was tied up in the hovel in which they sat – a hovel that nonetheless at the time of the boom was theoretically worth about eight hundred and fifty grand.

With a series of impressive flourishes, the advisor would sketch out a plan whereby the poor ould fella would 'release' the equity, going forward. This would enable him to 'live a little', in return for the bank having a grip on him that would ruin whatever was left of his existence – though the advisor wouldn't place too much emphasis on that last bit. In fact he wouldn't mention that, at all.

'Releasing the equity'. . . 'going forward'. . . such enticing words these, which had worked so well on the rest of the population, they could hardly fall to work on the most vulnerable. Even if they had no idea what it all meant, even if they hadn't been going in any direction except backwards for so long, that they didn't even have the vaguest notion of the outline of the concept of 'going forward'.

And to ensure the success of this part of the project, the independent financial advisor would explain that he would need to engage the services of the 'relevant professionals', meaning that he would collude with some local solicitor to clean out this particular homeowner good and proper. To put the poor ould fellas money to work for both of them.

In general the practice whereby members of the legal profession arrange the transfer of valuable assets from poor ould fellas to themselves and their associates is of such ancient origin in Ireland it could be described as our definitive national sport.

So naturally during the boom, it was played enthusiastically throughout the land. Thus it was, that a broken-down old cottage in some godforsaken part of the bog, might be advertised in *The Irish Times* as 'having splendid potential as a retreat for the artistically inclined', or 'an understated triumph of vernacular architecture, ripe with possibilities'.

The only slight problem was that the deal had to be concluded in such a way that the 'relevant professionals' received about 98 per cent of the money, while the poor ould fella, who was technically the owner and the sole beneficiary, would receive just about enough to pay the bus fare to his new lodgings in the County Home. And to cover the vet's bill for putting down Jack, because the County Home wouldn't allow him to keep a dog.

But, hey, it's every man for himself, as the independent financial advisors would say. '*Caveat emptor*', they would quip, the only words of Latin they would know, but enough to get them through a lifetime of defrauding those less fortunate than themselves.

And, as we have noted, they wouldn't even need to make some massive profit on the deal. Even if there was no 'equity' to be 'released', no house to be sold over the head of its rightful owner, nothing in it for their fellow 'professionals', the fact that they could get a poor ould fella to give them all the money he had under the bed, even if it was only a couple of thousand, nay, a couple of hundred, would be deeply satisfying to them.

It's the principle of the thing.

The World of Shops

Likes:

The shop in the village
  that closed down in
  1972

Dislikes:

Aldi

Lidl

Harvey Norman

Mobile phone shops

Avoca Handweavers

Louis Copeland

Curry's PC World

Any shop in any shopping centre

The Windmills of
Their Minds

In recent years in Ireland we have seen many protests on issues to do with the environment. In particular we have seen people proclaiming their opposition to the building of wind farms in their locality – they argue that the huge 'windmills' are giving off a low-frequency noise that is slowly driving them berserk, that they look terrible and that the ruination of the scenery that they cause is also destroying the values of property in the area.

These are all legitimate arguments made by people who have come together in a display of community spirit that is at once heart-warming and slightly confusing. Most of them, for example, are broadly in favour of harnessing the power of the wind and any other such measures that are good for the environment in general because they lessen our dependence on the burning of fossil fuels.

They are just against the way it is being done or, to be more precise, they are against the way it is being done to them. And while they are able to draw on a broad level of cross-community support for their disputes, there is one section of the community which is not to be seen on these protests – we'll give you a hint: they tend to be male and quite advanced in years and lacking in material wealth. And one more thing – they tend not to give a fuck.

So overwhelmed are the poor ould fellas by feelings of futility in the face of the profound corruption and other abuses to which they have been subjected all their lives, they have long since lost any desire to resist; they find it hard enough just to go on living – not that they had a very strong desire to resist in the first place, or indeed to live.

Given their allotted place in the great scheme, you would not blame them really, when they see a massive wind farm being built beside them and think: *Ah well, it could be worse.*

Because they are right; they know that it really could be worse. If the usual protocols were being followed, a bulldozer would simply have appeared one day in the yard and the poor ould fella would have been informed that the wind farm was going to be replacing his poor ould farm, and of course the poor ould farmhouse, which was about to be knocked down whether or not he was still inside it.

Yes, they usually find that their property rights and all other rights besides have been eroded over the years without them knowing much about it, so if someone decided to build a wind farm beside them, they are naturally grateful that it wasn't actually built on top of them. After that, they can usually adjust to the other hardships, in time.

The constant low-frequency noise that will drive other people berserk will probably not be heard to any extent by the more elderly in the community, who have already been driven berserk anyway by so many other things which Ireland has inflicted on them. And even if they could hear it, they might regard it as being preferable to listening to *The Ryan Tubridy Show* on the radio.

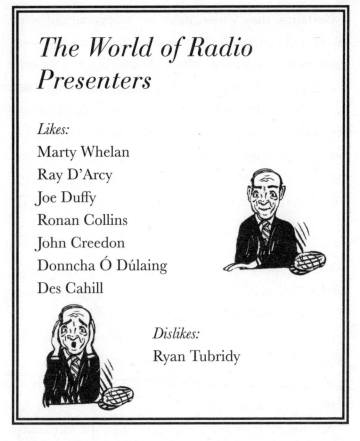

The World of Radio Presenters

Likes:
Marty Whelan
Ray D'Arcy
Joe Duffy
Ronan Collins
John Creedon
Donncha Ó Dúlaing
Des Cahill

Dislikes:
Ryan Tubridy

Yes, their property values may be ruined by the imposition of this giant structure which dominates the landscape, but then these men were not really planning to get into the property game anyway. It's not like most of them can 'trade down' – from where they are sitting, there is no down.

Certainly they would have been approached over the years by crooked estate agents, trying to convince them that they should sell the hovel they are in, buy a cheaper one and 'take a profit' – of course the estate agent will neglect to mention that the hovel of the poor ould fellas is in fact situated in an area of outstanding natural beauty, which makes it worth far more than the poor ould fella would appreciate, and far, far more than what the agent is telling him it is worth. So essentially the estate agent would be buying it for the view.

For the poor ould fella, the view has ceased to matter for a very long time. He just can't see the point of moving from this place to some other place, an even worse place, going to all that trouble just to 'downsize', as the fellow says. And for what? A few measly euro that the fellow and a few other fellows will soon chisel away, as is their wont?

No, the poor ould fellas are never to the fore when conversation turns to the issue of property values – this is one of life's anxieties at least that they have been spared. So when their neighbours are protesting on these grounds, they are conspicuous by their absence.

And as for the argument that they weren't properly consulted before the building of the wind farm, while that may be a valid argument for regular folks, the poor ould fellas wouldn't know what you were talking about.

Properly consulted? It is fair to say that the poor ould fellas are not consulted about any matter that has any bearing on their lives, in any shape or form, be it properly or improperly. At no point in any process or procedure in this country does anyone feel the slightest obligation to be consulting poor ould fellas on any aspect of what is being proposed. Indeed they wouldn't even do it just for a bit of amusement.

But they would be consulted if some interested party felt that he could take advantage of them – by trying to sell them a solar heating system, for example.

To the poor ould fella there might be a brief moment of hope here, as the solar heating brings to mind the solar farm. Which is an idea that the poor ould fella likes, because he saw the farm of someone in the next townland being turned into a solar farm, and it looks to him like nothing more than a load of glass that just sits there with the sun shining on it, for the few minutes of the year that the sun shines in these parts. It looks like the sort of thing you'd get a grant for, or money from the EEC, some kind of a deal anyway in which the farmer does nothing and still gets money for it – ah but that would be too easy, that would be far too good a thing to happen to a poor ould fella now, and deep down he knows it.

No, for this particular pantomime, one of the modern lads would call to the house of his prospective victim, who would duly let him in, for fear of what might happen if he didn't. And then he would have to listen to this person trying to sell him the solar heating – not to give him money for the solar farm, but to take it away with the solar heating.

The modern lad would insist that he is 'not going to waste your time', which is puzzling to the poor ould fella, who has nothing going on in his life but time. Anyway it is a lie, because the modern lad will waste all the time that he needs to bamboozle his host with talk of the savings he can make in the long term, if he installs these solar panels in the roof of the house.

This is even more puzzling to the poor ould fella, for whom there is no long-term, and probably not much of short-term either. But the modern lad just sees this as a challenge to his ingenuity, as he talks of things such as the health benefits of the solar panels, how much warmer the poor ould fella will be and how this could help him to live so much longer than the experts would have him believe – he will also be illustrating his

proposal by writing various bits of bullshit on a sheet of paper and joining them up with arrows. He will speak of 'front-loading' the payments, he will harry and he will cajole.

Finally he will make an appeal to the poor ould fella's sense of the greater good, of the future of humanity, he will ask him to look at 'the big picture'.

To the poor ould fella, who has been looking at nothing more than a big picture of the Sacred Heart for many years, this is not easy. As he listens to the modern lad describing the effects of climate change, the melting of the polar ice caps and so forth, and the urgent need to harness alternative sources of energy for the salvation of the earth and of mankind itself, his mind begins to drift back over the years to other such situations, in which bad men were trying to sell him things that he didn't want or didn't need. And in his mind he begins to formulate a response to the modern lad, who is still babbling on about 'renewables'.

The response goes something like this: 'Down all the days I have heard a fair amount of bullshit. Aye, they all come down here with their bullshit, be it the 'independent financial advisors' or the lads with the tarmacadam or the one looking for the vote at election time. But to be sitting here listening to this talk about the future of the human race depending on me, a poor ould fella, spending money I don't have on this new system that I don't want, due to the fact that I will very soon be dead . . . now that is bullshit of a kind I have never heard before, and Lord knows, I've heard some . . . aye, I've heard some.'

Yes, that is the speech he is preparing in his poor ould head, but he does not deliver it. Instead when the modern lad hands him a lovely fountain pen and shows him where to write his name, his mind goes a bit blank and the next thing he knows, he's signed his name and the modern lad is pumping his hand and congratulating him on what a great call he has made.

For himself, for Ireland and for the world.

For fuck's sake.

The Politics

For much of their lives, just about the only form of entertainment that the poor ould fellas knew was the politics. Whenever there was an election there was usually a bit of excitement to be had – 'excitement' in this case meaning perhaps a visit from a TD or even a minister to the house, to ask for the poor ould fella's vote and to listen to his problems, which would be solemnly written down in a little notebook by the candidate or one of his assistants, all parties to these proceedings being aware at all times that this was an entirely meaningless ceremony.

But they did it anyway, for, shall we say, presentational purposes. It just felt better than the truth, which would have involved listening to the poor ould fella's problems and then responding thus: 'I hear what you're saying, poor ould fella, but I'm obviously not going to do anything about it, because people like you don't matter a fuck to people like me. Now if you could just give me your vote and stop wasting my fucking time here, we can move on to the next hovel.'

No, such a response, while it would have been a perfectly accurate description of the innermost nature of the transaction taking place, might have looked bad to any passing reporters, and might even have caused a further delay in the candidate's busy schedule as the issues were fully ventilated.

So just to save time, the ritual of the writing down of the constituent's problems would be observed – though if a comprehensive list of the problems of the poor ould fellas were to be compiled, they would need a very big notebook, one of the A4-sized variety, ideally in hardback, with the word 'jumbo' on it. And they would need to cancel the rest of the day, at what is after all their busy time.

Still, the visit of the campaigners, while it would be of no material benefit, would help to break the monotony of life, for a few moments at least. And as the great day of the election drew near, there might be an even bigger visit to the area by a minister or even the party leader, who would be standing on the back of a lorry in the market square of the nearest town delivering a speech to his unfortunate followers.

For this a poor ould fella might get on the ould bike and make his way into the town, perhaps just for the sense of occasion that it offered – the speech itself

The World of Politicians

Likes:
Barack Obama
Mary McAleese
Mick Wallace (bit of a
  character)
Simon Harris (he was
  never young, really)
The late Liam Cosgrave

Dislikes:
Mary Lou McDonald
Michael and Danny Healy-Rae
  (rich ould fellas wearing the
  traditional costume of the poor ould fellas)
Trump
Boris Johnson
Nigel Farage
Any of those Brexit fuckers

would be of no merit, it would comprise the usual rancid assortment of baseless accusations and vainglorious ravings and obvious untruths, but the main speaker and his minions would present a formidable spectacle to the assembled gathering of corrupt local representatives and intoxicated rural cretins.

The crowd would probably be warmed up by a PA system blaring out terrible music, some nightmarish morass of country 'n' Irish and mawkish folk ballads celebrating the many war crimes of notorious republican terrorists, but at least it would bring a bit of 'life' to the old place, which had otherwise been quiet enough since it was the scene of some minor fracas during the 1798 Rebellion.

And then the big chief would be introduced, looking quite majestic to this crowd in a pin-striped suit – it might even be Charles J. Haughey himself, exuding what his simpleton followers would regard as a kind of charisma, though they would mutter darkly to one another that he had perhaps not achieved all that he had wished for in political life, because he had been 'crippled by the horn'.

Still, the roaring of these halfwits would send such a shiver down the spine of any vaguely civilised person, it would create a strange kind of energy. Which, disturbing though it would clearly be, felt slightly better than what everyone was used to, which was no energy, nothing at all.

Thus the poor ould fellas would get a small bit of enjoyment out of these otherwise grotesque episodes; they would find some mild form of diversion in the heathen fervour that would be whipped up by the fellows on the back of the lorry.

But they don't come down any more, those disgraceful men, they stopped doing the old roadshows around the time that television made it easier for them to 'get their message across', that message being the usual rancid assortment of baseless accusations and vainglorious ravings and obvious untruths . . . in that at least they remain consistent.

So the swift bout of bullshit at the doorstep, the briefest of brief encounters, is all that the poor ould fellas will be getting, and after that they'll have to try and follow it all on RTÉ. Which is not easy betimes, for men who were formed in a more impersonal age, one in which a taoiseach of the calibre of Seán Lemass would express no views of any description on matters pertaining to his private life, and certainly not to the more esoteric aspects of it, such as his sexual orientation.

There was no sexual orientation in the time of Lemass, and as regards his 'personality' in general, the only thing anyone knew about him was that he enjoyed a game of cards – but then nearly everyone in Ireland at that time enjoyed a game of cards, because there was fuck all else to be doing apart from winning pennies off each other in games of pontoon. Indeed many games were played for no money – because there was no money – just for a few Maguire & Paterson matches or some such form of pretend currency, which in no way diminished the pleasure of the games, given that there was virtually no pleasure in them anyway.

So that was about all that was known of your Seán Lemass or your Frank Aiken other than a vague awareness than in a previous phase of their careers they had undoubtedly murdered quite a few people, during Ireland's quest to be free. But no one thought to mention these things, any probings into such controversies were considered to be disrespectful and intrusive and a descent into issues of personality rather than policy.

What a surprise it is therefore, to the poor ould fellas, to be listening to Leo Varadkar on the radio telling Miriam O'Callaghan that he is gay. Previous leaders of Fine Gael such as Liam Cosgrave were not gay, but they were not openly heterosexual either. They were just . . . Liam Cosgrave.

As in all matters of a sexual nature, on this one the poor ould fellas are utterly indifferent. They really couldn't give less of a fuck about this, or about any other aspect of the inner life of Leo Varadkar. As we have already observed, their record of being non-judgemental on LGBTQI issues in general is exemplary, and they are not going to change that just because a gay man somehow becomes leader of Fine Gael. Mostly they just want to know if he's going to repeal the smoking ban (he is not, of course) or if he is going to make any other aspect of their lives just a small bit easier (again, no) or even if he is a supporter of the reinstatement of Johnny McEvoy to a prominent place in Irish culture (never heard of the man), so Leo's thoughts on life, love and personal growth will not really engage their enthusiasm to the full.

On balance they welcome the arrival of a gay taoiseach, because given all that they have endured from the other kind, they probably need a bit of a rest from the 'straight' community in general. But still they find it a bit strange when they hear a man on television talking about his husband; they assume that they must have missed something, that this is just a sign that their poor ould brains aren't working any more.

Not that they care about this either, but still it is one of those little signals that tells them the world is getting a bit complicated for the likes of them – they are hearing about that poor ould fella who went to the wedding of his grand-niece, only to find that she was getting married to a woman. They are not fit for such surprises, they're just not able for that sort of thing any more.

But if Leo Varadkar does get married to his partner, they hope that it will all work out roughly the way that it did for Seán Lemass and his wife, or Liam Cosgrave and his wife, with the partner in question adopting a 'low-key' approach, so low, indeed, as to be totally invisible to the point where nobody is aware that they ever existed on this earth in any shape or form.

But they know too that that old world is dying, that public figures don't have the inhibitions they used to, that they don't think it's a good idea any more to be emotionally stunted and to be trapped in dead relationships – things that were once regarded not just as desirable in a leader but almost compulsory for any man hoping to oversee the effective conduct of the affairs of state.

And the poor ould fellas have also noted that at the end of all this new-found freedom of expression, there is Donald Trump. Often they do be sitting on the couch with Jack the poor ould dog, looking at Trump on the television, and even poor ould Jack starts to get a bit anxious in himself, a bit upset.

He does start whimpering and he hops off the couch and starts pawing at the door, as if the voice of Trump and all the shit that he's talking is setting off something in Jack, bringing him back to some ancient trauma. To Jack's master, Trump is equally disconcerting, everything he says amounts to those two overly familiar words which now seem to dominate what is left of the poor ould fella's days: Stop relaxing . . . stop relaxing . . . stop relaxing.

There would often be a picture of John F. Kennedy in the house of a poor ould fella, and sometimes he would look at this vision of excellence and then he would look at Trump roaring and shouting on the television, and he would ponder the infinite magnitude of human folly.

He would think back to the nights when the leader of Fianna Fáil might be standing on the back of the lorry in the middle of the town, ranting at a large collection of the local morons, telling his lies with an enthusiasm that bordered on the pathological, as if he was trying to win a bet against some other pathological liar who had set up in the next town, to see which of them could tell the most lies in the shortest amount of time, to see which one of them was the crookedest fucker, the most profoundly dishonest person in the region or even in the whole country at that time.

When the poor ould fella looks at Trump, he harks back to those men on those nights on the back of those lorries and he thinks, *You know . . . maybe they weren't the worst.*

And he wonders if, without knowing it back then, he might even have been happy.

THE
INTERNET
AND ALL THAT

Modern Technology

For the poor ould fellas, the internet should be a boon.

In theory at least, it should enable them to engage with the world in ways that may actually be to their benefit – as distinct from most of the ways in which they engage with the world, which are of course to their detriment.

Yes, in theory . . .

In theory, for example, they should be able to derive some benefit from the invention of online gambling because they find it increasingly difficult or just unpleasant to be in a betting office with its ultramodern accoutrements and of course its prohibition on smoking.

The huge banks of screens that they find in these emporia are to them like some alien vision of a demented amusement arcade, so different to the old offices of the turf accountant in which there was . . . not much, really.

But there was enough, indeed there was more than enough in those modest old premises to assist the poor ould punter in making his selections. Basically there were pages torn out of the racing sections of the papers and stuck to the walls, along with more detailed cuttings from the specialist organs such as *The Sporting Life*.

And they could be perused in peace, a peace that came partly from the fact that the turf accountant's office would be situated in an unpopular part of the town and would have darkened windows to stop people looking in, to discourage those who were merely seeking this thing they call 'fun'.

It was a peace broken only by the sounds of quiet conversation on the part of the aficionados, or by the voice of the English lady on the Extel service who provided commentaries on the races. Indeed there would usually be nothing but races, just horse races; there would be no betting on clay-court tennis matches in Bulgaria or on who would score first in the Monday Night Football featuring Watford and Huddersfield. There would be no live pictures of greyhound races at eleven o'clock in the morning, there would be no screens offering prices on the Super Bowl, there would be no comfortable seats and there would definitely be no water cooler.

Of all the bullshit developments that the poor ould

fellas have seen, the arrival of the water cooler would be up there in the very front rank. It's not just the fact that nobody used to need to drink water, and now everyone needs to do it, all the time – it's the fact that someone thought it was a great idea to stop the poor ould fellas from smoking while they were having their few shillings each way on the horses, but to provide them with unlimited quantities of water.

Yes, that was a great exchange there, that was an excellent deal – no doubt they conducted extensive research on that one, putting together focus groups comprising a representative selection of poor ould fellas in order to create a betting office environment that would best serve the needs and desires of the more elderly clientele going forward.

No doubt the big question was put to them: 'Would you prefer (a) to be able to smoke while you're having your bet as you always have done or (b) to be given access to a supply of chilled water, in a paper cup?' And then the supplementary question: 'If (b) is your choice, would you prefer still or sparkling?'

I mean, they'd hardly just bring in something that would take away about 97 per cent of the pleasure of the experience from the poor ould fellas, would they? Nah, they'd never do that, surely? They'd check with them first, before making that executive decision which would mean they would have to stand smoking in the cold and the rain outside the turf accountant's office, which now had all the good things about turf accountants' offices taken out . . . ah, yes, they'd run that one by the poor ould fellas, wouldn't they?

Anyway, however it happened, it is now almost unknown to see a poor ould fella in a betting office, a place that to him was once a natural habitat, a sanctuary, next to the pub in which he could contemplate the day's card at Newbury in the pages of the *Irish Press* – before they destroyed that for him too.

But in theory – ah, yes, in theory – he should be able to partake of some sort of vaguely agreeable betting experience by logging on to his online account with Paddy Power or bet365 on his laptop.

Unfortunately there are certain, shall we say, challenges that present themselves in this otherwise splendid scenario. In the first place, in order to 'access' your online betting account you have to be able to open one in the first place and for that you will need some form of credit card or an equivalent form of plastic money. And in these matters the poor ould fella tends to be something of a traditionalist, favouring actual money in notes and coins, rather than the card that to him is alien.

Not that this would be an entirely insurmountable problem if there weren't other speed bumps to be negotiated on this particular journey – the main one being that since the poor ould fellas live in 'rural Ireland', there is a very good chance that they don't have broadband, so that even if they wanted it, there is no internet that they can 'access'.

And there probably never will be.

This arose out of the enlightened government policy of placing these matters of telecommunications and other vital national interests in the care of business people rather than just letting the state do it – because the private sector gets these things done a lot better, doesn't it?

Yes, it's much better to hand over that whole broadband thing to people whose only interest in it is to make money out of it, rather than let the old state make a complete balls of everything as usual. I mean, imagine if they hadn't brought the spirit of free enterprise to the task of hooking Ireland up to the internet – for all we know, large parts of 'rural Ireland' might still be unconnected, with potentially catastrophic consequences for its inhabitants, not least the poor ould fellas who would be unable to open an online betting account – if they had a credit card.

Ah, it was a great day's work all the same, throwing that one out to the business community. And as they were making their executive decisions about which parts of the country should have the broadband and which parts should have very little band at all, imagine our surprise that the latter just happen to be the parts which contain the overwhelming majority of poor ould fellas.

No, you couldn't have seen that one coming, not in a million years. Which is not to say that the internet is a good thing and that everyone should have it. On the contrary, it is clearly a very bad thing in many ways and, as we will be observing, the poor ould fellas can consider themselves fortunate to be excluded from it, for the most part.

But in this one area – the online gambling – they could have used it. In the unlikely event that by some strange accident they had the broadband in their locality, and in the even more unlikely event that they possessed a credit card, they could be sitting there enjoying a relaxing smoke, opening up the laptop and entering their username and password into their bet365 account to peruse the afternoon's fare at Newton Abbot. If they could remember their username and password, a feat that of course they would not be

guaranteed to accomplish on every occasion. Not 100 per cent certain that one.

Especially as they would be required to have slightly different passwords for different online betting providers, with some of them insisting on all lower-case letters, some demanding at least one digit, and so on.

But if somehow they got over that obstacle, they would be nicely set up there, opening the laptop in order to log on to their online account and to wager the few shillings . . . were it not for the fact that being poor ould fellas, almost by definition, they wouldn't have a laptop.

It is just not their style, to be dropping in to the computer store in the nearest town, to spend €700 on a new laptop – €400 for the computer itself, and an extra €300 thrown in by the owner to take advantage of their innocence. No, you don't see many poor ould fellas cycling home from the town carrying a large box emblazoned with the legend Packard Bell, anxious to get home as quickly as possible so that they can read the instructions – no problem there, you may be sure – and set it up and immediately join LinkedIn to do a bit of networking with other poor ould fellas.

No, that would not be an everyday sight on the internet-free roads of 'rural Ireland'.

So, yes indeed, 'twould be a fine thing if the poor ould fellas could open their laptops and log on to their online betting accounts in order to start betting courtesy of their friends at Mastercard. But since no part of this arrangement would be within their comfort zone or even their discomfort zone or any other zone they might inhabit evidently it is just not meant to be.

And thus the only section of the community for whom online gambling might be a good thing is effectively barred from entering that arena.

It is perhaps some consolation that they have absolutely no knowledge of any of this, not the remotest idea, and that even if it were carefully explained to them, they still would not have a clue.

Which is one small mercy at least that the good Lord in His wisdom has bestowed on them.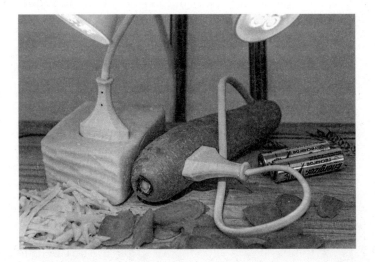

A World Full of No

The poor ould fellas are vaguely aware that there is a debate going on in the outside world about the internet, with considerable concern being expressed about the manifold problems it is creating and its potential to bring most forms of civilised life on earth to a close.

They hear voices on the wireless speaking of things that they do not understand, and yet they can pick up the gist of what they are saying – that most people in that outside world are now hopelessly addicted to this internet and that they would very much like to break that addiction but fear that if they do, they would have no idea how to go on living.

All told, from what they can gather, the poor ould fellas are somewhat relieved that they have dodged this particular bullet. They can hardly believe it actually, given that they have been shot full of holes, as it were, in every other engagement with the enemy, which is everywhere.

Imagine their surprise, then, that as they strain

their poor ould ears to catch another of these radio discussions on the massively destructive force that is the world wide web, they find that they are being encouraged by their 'carers' to learn how to use it, to sign up for it, to get involved.

How strange, they think, that they have been perhaps the only people on earth to avoid this plague, yet now they are being encouraged to sign up for a dose of it, by those who by their own admission are googling their lives away.

Aye, that's a good one, that's a funny thing – or at least it would be if the poor ould fellas could allow themselves a laugh at these little ironies they are always encountering. Indeed if it was happening to someone else and not to them, they really would be seeing all the humour inherent in it and appreciating it in all its cosmic absurdity.

Alas, it is happening to them, the way that everything else happens to them whether they like it or not. Usually it is some otherwise well-intentioned person from the social services who is trying to lead them down the information superhighway, dragging them out of their homes and into a minibus filled with other poor ould fellas bound for the community hall and a grand old session about how this internet can change their lives.

The World of Modern Technology

Likes:
Television
Radio

Dislikes:
Smartphones
Electric cars
The internet
Wind farms
Pay-per-view television
Plastic money
Vaping
And all other forms of modern technology

Immediately we can see the tragic flaw here: the belief that these men might have the remotest interest in changing their lives to learn how to live like the modern lads.

'You won't know yourselves,' they are told by these disturbingly optimistic young people, who seem quite unaware that it can already be said of quite a few of the poor ould fellas that they don't know themselves. That they can be looking into the mirror for quite some time, for even a few hours at a stretch, wondering who on earth that strange old man looking back at them is and what he wants.

Eventually they conclude that most likely he wants the same things they want, which is very, very little – and that, like them, he has absolutely no chance of getting it.

But they do have some inkling of how the modern lads are living, how they are always on the internet in what used to be a cosy lounge, but is now a sports bar with forty big screens showing top Premier League action and a sign that says 'Wi-Fi Available'. A sign that tells the poor ould fellas that they obviously have no idea what Wi-Fi is, they know only that it is not for them.

It is for the modern lads, who use these new words that are mostly incomprehensible to anyone born before 1950, some of which lodge themselves anyway even in the most elderly of minds.

'Apps' is a big one.

They hear a lot of this muttering about the 'apps', and they understand that there is an app for almost everything that the human heart desires, which makes the poor ould fellas wonder if there might be an app that would bring Johnny McEvoy on to RTÉ some afternoon, singing 'The Boston Burglar'.

Would there be any chance at all of finding that one in the App Store? Are you telling us there wouldn't? No Johnny McEvoy in the afternoon on RTÉ singing 'The Boston Burglar' app? Oh what a surprise that is. No doubt this is an oversight that will be corrected right away.

Or maybe it will not be corrected, at least not in time for the poor ould fellas and maybe not even in time for Johnny himself, unless somehow he ends up living to the age of a hundred and ninety-three.

So that would be another no, then, no such app, or indeed no app of any kind that would answer the needs of the poor ould fellas, in this world full of no.

As for the one other app that they need most desperately, the app that could bring them in out of the cold and the rain to enjoy a relaxing smoke along with their glass of stout in what used to be a cosy bar, that is an app so unattainable, you might as well be talking about an app that would send you flying in your own custom-built rocket ship to the dark side of the moon.

But not to worry, there are these enthusiastic young social workers taking that minibus load of poor ould fellas to the community hall to talk to them about things like 'social media', which, they explain, can compensate in many ways for not having a social life, as such. Or indeed any kind of life.

In these bright, airy surroundings the audience for this lecture is feeling quite uncomfortable, as they much preferred the old hall, which was built in 1926 and which would still do them fine, even though it now has nettles growing in it, and there is no Wi-Fi available.

Indeed, that is now seeming like quite a bonus, as they sit there listening to this person talking to them about the fucking internet.

Yes, the person is talking, and telling them that there is an excellent Wi-Fi signal here in the community hall, to which they are welcome at all times, if they wish to acquire some basic computer skills that they wouldn't be able to use at home because there would be no point, given that there is no broadband, no Wi-Fi, no hot spots, no access to the internet in any shape or form, no nothing.

Still the person is talking and effectively he is talking in a foreign language. It's as if he is talking in French, to a crowd that knows no French, who can only make out these odd words that are vaguely recognisable but essentially meaningless – 'broadband' . . . 'modem' . . . 'Wi-Fi'.

Indeed, the only thing that is sticking in the minds of the poor ould fellas is that they can't accept that Wi-Fi is pronounced 'wye-fye' and not 'wiffy', as it was pronounced by the Senator Fidelma Healy-Eames during a major speech in the Seanad about . . . something or other.

A traditionalist she may be, but for the poor ould fellas Healy-Eames got it right first time there, with the 'wiffy', and as far as they are concerned, whatever the modern lads are calling it, 'wiffy' it is and 'wiffy' it always will be.

Other words from the new lexicon of cyberspace dance across their minds and then keep on dancing until they are there no more.

Facebook comes up a number of times. This otherwise helpful individual is trying to explain what

Facebook is, to these men who have been around roughly since the time of Christ and therefore would have a limited appetite for 'friending' or 'unfriending' others of their ilk, or anyone else for that matter.

Certainly the modern world has 'unfriended' them in a major way, but they have no desire to reciprocate, no desire to be 'reaching out' either and absolutely no idea what is meant by a 'status update'.

They have no status.

There is nothing to add to that and there never has been and there never will be, so there is nothing to be 'updated' there. We can safely say that a situation will not arise whereby a poor ould fella will be contemplating his status and forming the opinion that it has changed in some way from what it was yesterday or the day before or the fourteen years before that.

He will not be 'updating' it to let us know that he is taking in the Monaco Grand Prix for a few days, he will be where he always is, except on the days when he is forced to be in the community hall, listening to this shit about upping his social-media game in general or about how to describe himself in his Facebook profile – 'in a relationship' would not be featuring here. 'Single' would probably cover it, but then 'single' sometimes carries the inherent suggestion that this is a temporary situation, whereas of course in this case it is perhaps the only truly permanent thing that mankind has ever known.

Not that any of this will happen anyway, due to that language barrier that means that the poor ould fella is hearing nothing but these isolated words, that could mean anything, but which to him sound like they couldn't ever mean anything good.

There is just one thing that gets the attention of every man present, that gives this whole internet racket some resonance in their souls. In an aside, as if it were a matter of no importance, the speaker quips that the internet has a lot of pictures of dogs on it. That people are always 'posting' the latest antics of their loveable hounds. There are pictures of cats too, but it is the dogs that fire the enthusiasm of the poor ould fellas.

For this one thing, for these millions of pictures of Jack the dog and all the other dogs who would also be called Jack if they had anything to do with it, for one moment – just the most fleeting of moments – it seems to the poor ould fellas that all the trouble caused by this bastarding internet might nearly be worth it.

Nearly . . . but not quite.

The World of Comedy

Likes:
D'Unbelievables
Pat Shortt
Jon Kenny

Dislikes:
Al Porter

Off the Grid

When we see another person sitting on a park bench, taking the sun or perhaps smoking a relaxing cigarette outside a pub, we will usually have very little idea what is going on in their heads. There is this mysterious and ungovernable element to human affairs, based on the fact that we never truly know what someone else is thinking, and in some cases we would probably be amazed if we were to find out.

And while this law of nature may apply even to the poor ould fellas up to a point, in their case there are two things to be borne in mind – it's not so much that nobody knows what's going on their heads rather that nobody cares. And unlike the situation as it pertains to most other people, we have a very definite idea of the things that are NOT going on in the heads of the poor ould fellas.

For example, no poor ould fella anywhere, at any time, will be putting his mind to the task of composing a tweet. They have been spared this, somehow; they have many things to be worrying them, but finding the form of words that will most concisely express their point of view on Twitter is not one of them.

So that's one thing we can rule out completely.

Nor would they be thinking about trolling someone who has displeased them or about re-tweeting an article on the problem of rural isolation or about sending a DM to some other poor ould fella or about unfollowing Donald Trump.

These are other things they won't be doing. Of that you can be sure.

They will not be scrolling down their timelines to keep abreast of developments in the Premier League transfer window, they will not be scrolling down anything.

Nor will they be wondering how the other members of their WhatsApp group are feeling about great issues of the day, you can take that to the bank. Indeed, most of the things that other people are thinking about all the time are things that never enter the heads of the poor ould fellas because of course they do not possess smartphones.

As a result, it will be a rare member of the tribe who will be thinking, *You know, I think I'll take a picture of my dinner and post it on the old twitter-machine.* Indeed, since the invention of social media there must have been a hundred million postings of dinners, not one of which was put there by the elderly men in whom we are primarily interested, and not just because they don't have smartphones – even if they did, they would be constrained from sharing images of their evening meals by the fear that they would be mocked by the modern lads.

A few boiled potatoes may be more than enough for their delicate stomachs to digest, and indeed they might even congratulate themselves for getting through such an ordeal, but such a presentation would hardly pass muster with the highly sophisticated audience

with whom they would be connecting: 'Hey, old timer, if you put a fucking sausage on there you might even nail that third Michelin star!', they will taunt.

Nor would a bowl of oxtail soup and a few slices of Galtee processed cheese between slices of white Irish Pride bread be likely to draw a rave review from the random commentator online: 'Hey, you old bastard, I was going to post a moussaka dish that I developed from an original concept by Marco Pierre White but I see you've got to the cutting edge of international cuisine before me, you geriatric fuck!'

So even if they had smartphones, posting pictures of their dinners would not be the smart play. The fact that they are outside that particular loop, no more than all the other loops, merely renders impossible something that would be undesirable anyway – which is about the best break they'll be getting, all round.

Indeed, while some will celebrate life, liberty and the pursuit of happiness, for the poor ould fellas being incapable of doing something that would only be unpleasant for them anyway is the closest they will get to A Result.

The voices of the bourgeoisie will say, 'And could they not be taught how to use the smartphone, for the manifold benefits it could bring them?' The same voice, you will recall, that wonders why on earth they can't just have a nice cup of coffee in the cosy lounge bar instead of a nice glass of stout.

Well, no, they could not be taught how to use the smartphone because they've got this natural reluctance to have all the bullshit of the modern world crammed into one small object that they are obliged to carry with them at all times. How do they know that it's bullshit?

Let's just say they have made an educated guess. Let's just say that it is not just the hipsters who have stumbled across this intuition about what a smartphone can bring to your life, even if you had a life. It is the hipsters and the poor ould fellas – albeit coming at

it from somewhat different perspectives – and the hipsters would concede that the old-fashioned mobile phone, the dumbphone, might have its uses, while the poor ould fellas on this, too, would demur.

Rarely will you see them ambling down the street smiling to themselves as they send an amusing text to one of their good buddies, not for them the loud conversation on the mobile that everyone else on the bus can hear – such sights and sounds from the poor ould fellas are not to be found in our world.

Not only are they off the grid, they are off the grid, turn right and keep going, keep going . . . keep going . . . just keep going.

And while there may be a slight downside in terms of connectedness, there is a certain logic to it. After all, since most of the functions of even the dumbphone are bewildering to them, how are they supposed to address the challenges of its much smarter relation, even if they *could* be arsed? How are they supposed to get their ould heads around concepts such as FaceTime? Should we not all be aspiring to leave out the interconnectedness-of-all-things and just shut the fuck up for a while?

But of the many images that Steve Jobs and his friends have carved into our consciousness, there is one above all the others from which the poor ould fellas are estranged – that would be the selfie.

They don't do selfies.

Not once, not for a moment, not even for an infinitesimal fraction of a millisecond has the thought popped into the mind of such a man that what he'd really like to do now is take out the old iPhone and take a picture of himself and send it to some other poor ould fella for reasons neither of them would understand.

Perhaps there is some ancient wisdom in this, a sense that when a person has their photograph taken they lose some part of their soul – and if they happen to be taking the photograph themselves, perhaps they have no soul in the first place to lose.

Certainly it is a brand of wisdom not exclusive to the poor ould fellas, but it is one of their more salient characteristics, or non-characteristics, another of those things that they will never, ever be thinking about and certainly never doing.

The selfie and of course the selfie stick have no place in their lives. They will not be taking pictures of themselves nor will they be taking pictures of themselves with other people having a great time on some big night out.

No, that ain't going to happen either. For some strange reason you never really see a poor ould fella at, say, the BAFTA awards, so it follows that you are unlikely to see him in a group shot with Benedict Cumberbatch and Jude Law and Emma Watson, and you will certainly not see him photo-bombing any such group, celebrating the simple joy of being alive in this raucous fashion.

SHOPPING LIST
MILK
BREAD
TEA
RASHERS
T. PAPER
NEWSPAPER
SPUDS
RAT POISON
ANADIN
T. KETCHUP

That is not his way, the glittering gala occasion is not for him. But even in real life you're never going to see anything like this, you're never going to see a poor ould fella in the cosy lounge bar, quietly taking his iPhone out of his inside pocket and photographing himself so that he will be able to preserve something of these transient moments of modest pleasure – on the whole, his aim is to preserve as little as possible of what is left to him, he just wants it all to be over.

All of his instincts rise up against this keeping of photographic souvenirs, understandably so when you consider that men of his generation would have been photographed no more than twice in the first sixty-five years of life, ideally without them knowing anything about it. And as for the process of selecting the 'best' selfie from the many taken, no, let us just say that that would not be their forte.

No, they would not be agonising about the camera-phone capturing their most attractive side, they would not be striking that pose they had been practising for so long in the mirror, they would not be conscious of projecting an image of themselves, of creating their own brand, as it were.

None of these things exist for them in any form. They are free of all such thoughts, free in ways that other men are not free – if only they knew it.

The Content

A while back, the poor ould fellas started hearing this word being used, that had never been used before, at least not in the way it was now being used.

The word was 'content'.

Most days they'd be listening to the wireless and one of the modern lads would be using this word, to describe things it had never described before, things like an article in the paper or a television programme or something you'd find on a computer – indeed the social worker in the community hall was always mentioning that there was some great 'content' to be had on the internet.

The way it was pronounced, it sounded to the poor ould fellas like they were leaving out the 's' at the end, that it should be 'contents', the word you'd see on a tin of peas or a tin of beans, to describe well, the contents.

The 'contents' of a tin of peas, usually, were peas. The 'contents' of a tin of beans, usually, were beans. It was a kind of a statement of the obvious, just a way of describing in the most basic way what was inside some container, be it a can or a box or a bag of flour.

Now, it seemed to the poor ould fellas, it was changing. Now it was still being pronounced the same way, but it wasn't plural any more, and this 'content' seemed to cover nearly everything that had words in it or pictures or any combination thereof.

Which gave the poor ould fellas a bit of a problem. Because they knew deep down that nothing that was called 'content' could be any good.

For example, they'd be thinking that *Knocknagow* by Charles Kickham could never be called 'content'. Or one of the collections of the writings of Con Houlihan – again, you couldn't call what was on those pages 'content'. Or maybe a good western, like *Stagecoach* – no, you wouldn't be calling that 'content' either. Or the great colour pictures of the two teams in the All-Ireland finals that the *Sunday Press* and *Sunday Independent* used to print as their front pages – would that have been content? No, it would not.

And the reason these things could not be called 'content' is that . . . now how could the poor ould fellas put this to avoid accusations of bias against the modern lads and their modern world? . . . OK, the reason, the only reason that these things could not be called content is that they were . . . good.

Or to put it another way – and I'm afraid there

really is no other way of putting this – to say that they were good is also to say that there is something they were not . . . and that something, which they were not, is this: they were NOT FUCKING SHIT.

Because when the poor ould fellas are listening to all this babble about 'content', after a while a strange thing happens and they are not hearing that word any more, they are starting to hear other words. Words like 'fucking' and 'shit'.

In that order.

So the modern lad is on *Morning Ireland*, maybe on the business news, saying something like this: 'We will be supplying premium content by creating a synergy of content in which creators of content can interact with other content creators across the spectrum in

order to focus on the generation of new content, more content going forward . . . '

The poor ould fella is hearing these words, but not quite in the way that they are being delivered. What he is hearing goes something like this: 'We will be supplying premium fucking shit, by creating a synergy of fucking shit in which creators of fucking shit can interact with other fucking shit creators across the spectrum in order to focus on the generation of new fucking shit, more fucking shit going forward . . . '

Or words to that effect.

He feels it could not be otherwise, that the modern lads by simply describing something as 'content', in this way, are taking away about 99 per cent of the chance of it being any good. And most likely they are doing this so that they can get it on the cheap.

Time was when you'd put that tin of peas beside that Con Houlihan book and you'd know that the 'contents' of one would be worth considerably less than the 'contents' of the other – that the tin of peas was filled with its contents after a mechanical procedure which involved little more than emptying the required amount of the substance into the container, hundreds of versions of the same thing all packed into the one place.

The Con Houlihan book, by contrast, was not

just the same few words dumped in large quantities between two covers, it did not just consist of quite a lot of the one thing. It was quite a lot of many different things – different words, different thoughts, different observations.

It was just a lot more complicated than any item of canned goods and, as a result, you would pay perhaps £10 for the Con Houlihan book and about 10p for the peas.

But if everything is just 'content', if you give the impression that there isn't much difference between one kind of content and any other kind, and if you give them all away free anyway on the internet, to the poor ould fellas you're taking all the good out of it.

Now of course they may be wrong about this. They may have formed this opinion that is ultimately unsupported by the evidence, they may be mistaken in their belief that the word 'content' is a kind of nuclear bomb intended by the bad people of the world to annihilate all considerations of quality or discrimination so that eventually all this 'content' can by 'created' by some unfortunate youth who will be happy to receive about $20 a year for the privilege.

Yeah, the poor ould fellas may be completely off the mark on that one, because as we know, your global

corporations are always looking for ways in which they can expand the frontiers of human creativity, in which they can find ways to suitably reward the individual for the quality of his work; indeed they are always worried that they're just not offering the multitudes a product that is good enough, worried even more that they're not paying everyone enough.

So in that analysis, yes, the poor ould fellas would be wrong to see the perversion of the word 'content' as a kind of a Manhattan Project aimed at obliterating an entire culture in which, once upon a time, some things were regarded as being better than other things.

But is there perhaps another analysis which might favour the perspective of the poor ould fellas here? Is there a valid point of view out there that says that they are not wrong about this but that they are right?

Well, put it like this: before newspapers started describing their articles as 'content', a poor ould fella could spend half the day trying to decide which one he should buy (which broadsheet, obviously), which one was best for Gaelic games, best for racing, best for farming news and the 'spot the ball' competitions of course – and then he would buy the one with Con Houlihan in it anyway.

But at least he could dally awhile, knowing that some good would come of it. Now he's in the newsagent's and there's no Con Houlihan any more, only little scraps of tabloids that wouldn't have enough space for a proper article, even if they had any inclination to print one, which they don't, only stories about some fellow from *EastEnders* who's after beating up some other fellow from *EastEnders*, and lads in Dublin going around shooting each other.

Likewise since the arrival of 'content' on television, mysteriously most of the good programmes seem to be gone. And again, the poor ould fellas would not insult the good ones that remain by calling them 'content' – Mary Kennedy on *Nationwide* is not 'content', she's just a nice type of woman, the friendly sort, unaffected by fame and fortune. Her co-presenter Anne Cassin, too, is very down to earth.

Vigilant though he may be, it's still hard for a poor oud fella to avoid the 'content'. He may be drifting off during the RTÉ news, unable to stay awake during another report from Syria, and he may accidentally knock the remote control so that it changes over to TV3, where *Xposé* might be going on.

That's 'content' there, that's definitely this thing they call content, but it could be called a lot of other things too. And there's no need for it really; if you can't take in the stuff from Syria, you can just do like the poor ould fellas and fall asleep, instead of being woken up by the loud music and the flashing lights of the catwalk.

The poor ould fellas may need a break from all the wars and the earthquakes no more than the next man, but it doesn't follow that they will feel any more relaxed looking at the catwalk. No, you won't be finding the poor ould fellas punching the air and hollering, 'Karl Lagerfeld has only nailed it again!', before returning with a heavy heart to the main evening news and the latest from the Trumper.

They don't necessarily want more of anything, they just want less of everything – no content at all, in fact, would be ideal.

STYLE AND LEISURE

Nivea for Men, Not for Poor Ould Fellas

In their own way, the poor ould fellas are trying to maintain certain standards in relation to what is broadly known as their 'appearance'.

They would never attend any appointment with a solicitor or a doctor wearing 'casual' clothes, partly because they don't possess any causal clothes. If you were to tell them that the dress code for an event was 'smart casual', they would have no idea what you were talking about, but then they would never be invited to such an event anyway, so it's hard to imagine why you'd be telling them about the dress code in the first place.

No, if they have to go to the solicitor to arrange to have certain lands or moneys stolen from them or to the doctor to be told how little time they have left to live, they will always try to pay some attention to their 'appearance', to wear the better of the two suits that have served them so faithfully down all the days. And they might even don their most recently acquired cap, maybe the one they wore to see the pope in Galway in

1979, as distinctive a statement in its own way as any form of African headdress.

In the consistency of their 'look', they are like the busy executive who wears a traditional black pin-striped suit to free up his thoughts for the day ahead and all the exciting corporate combat it will bring, without worrying about how he's looking – with the slight difference that for the ould fellas the day ahead promises nothing much, really, certainly nothing that could be called exciting. Unless your solicitor reducing your net worth by about 98 per cent with the stroke of a pen can be called exciting. Unless the doctor examining you and telling you there's absolutely no medical or scientific reason for you to be alive at all can be called exciting.

But it is in the area of what we might call male grooming that we see perhaps the greatest divergence between the ways of the poor ould fellas and those of other men.

Sometimes when they are half-asleep in front of the telly, half-looking at the ads, they see the one featuring the Liverpool footballer Adam Lallana promoting the Nivea for Men range of products. They are struck in particular by the existence of this thing called 'moisturiser', which to them seems very strange.

Moisturiser . . . what would you be doing with something like that? In some part of their diminishing consciousness they do have a sense of this 'moisturiser' being a kind of an ointment that the fellow would be rubbing in to his face, they can just about get that.

What they do not have a sense of, what they do not get, is why the fuck he would be doing such a thing.

More Bullshit

Craft beers
Craft gin
Eurovision allowing the
    people to vote
Dog grooming
Paddy Power ads
Expensive crisps
Electric cars
'Going online'
Stag parties
The Iona Institute
Golf

Where will they plug in the electric cars?

At what point in human history, they ask themselves, did men feel it necessary or even desirable to be moisturising their faces?

Well, in truth, they don't really ask that question in those precise terms, in truth they are just lost in bewilderment at the whole business. At no point in their lives, from their harsh upbringing to their equally harsh coming of age, to the harshest part of all, in which they became poor ould fellas, has it ever occurred to them that there might be some merit in the idea of using this thing called moisturiser – nay, in the idea of paying money in order to use a product of this nature.

Even if this thing called moisturiser was something that grew wild on the side of the road, like blackberries, they would have no use for it, or could see no reason why any other man would have a use for it. Indeed if someone came to the door with a year's supply of it, and just left it there along with a €5 note thanking them for their time and apologising for any inconvenience, the poor ould fellas still wouldn't go near it.

They are vaguely aware that it has something to do with making your face softer – but, again, as to why the fuck anyone would want to make his face softer, they have no answers. There are other products of this nature they have noted, such as this tube of something that is called 'face wash'. This, according to the manufacturers, 'gently removes impurities', and has '0% alcohol'.

A poor ould fella would be looking at that label for a long time and finding no consolation – are there men alive in the world today who are so free of cares and woe that they can spend actual money on gently removing the impurities in their faces? And as for the bit about it having no alcohol – at that point the last imaginable reason for going on that journey just slips away.

Then there's the further complication that the

Nivea for Men ads have Premier League footballers in them, which suggests to the poor ould fellas that these unnatural practices are rife among sportsmen in general, the sort of men who used to represent everything that moisturiser and face balm are not – hurling men like Christy Ring or Nicky Rackard or Eddie Keher, and giants of Gaelic football such as Jack Quinn or Mattie McDonagh or Paddy McCormack, the Iron Man from Rhode.

The modern reader might not be overly familiar with the life and work of Paddy McCormack, the Iron Man from Rhode, but suffice it to say that he didn't come by that name due to the huge amounts of moisturiser and face balm he could apply to his cheeks without flinching – no, that was not it, that was not it at all.

And it's not that the poor ould fellas are entirely immune to the charms of the purveyors of cosmetics. They would have had some awareness of the phenomenon of aftershave, they would recognise that it has some place in the greater scheme and in fact they still have a bottle of Old Spice somewhere in the house, a Christmas present they got from the grand-niece back in the 1970s.

Everyone was using the Old Spice back then, even

normal fellows. But now it's all the 'after-shave balm', all kinds of 'balm' really. The modern lads, they love the ould balm.

Then again they must have the faces cut off themselves with the razors they use. Once more, as he is drifting off to sleep, one sleep closer to the big one, the poor ould fella will see one of these ads for Gillette razors in which the blades nearly come through the television screen to attack him as he slumbers on his own couch.

He gets a terrible fright, until he realises it's only a razor they're trying to advertise, albeit one with what at first seems about fourteen blades in it. For the poor ould fella, the razor with one blade in it was always enough, scraping away at the lather applied with a shaving brush, not the foam that is sprayed from an aerosol can, which they have never really trusted. And indeed some of them are still using the one blade that they inserted into the razor around the time of the controversial Fine Gael–Labour coalition government led by Mr Liam Cosgrave, with Mr Brendan Corish – a decent man – as tánaiste.

Still, it seems to work for them, the single-blade job, whereas for the modern lads it seems that no amount of blades is ever enough – they can get four blades in the one razor now, whereas three was once thought to be the limit of human achievement in terms of the razor and before that the twin-blade was the big breakthrough.

Since they'll hardly be able to keep increasing the number of blades indefinitely, perhaps the poor ould fellas will live to see the day when a massive TV advertising campaign will declare that the only logical development is a return to the old single-blade method – then again it is equally likely that the poor ould fellas will not live to see that day, unless it happens very soon.

Whatever the future holds in that regard, already the poor ould fellas have become aware of men using razors for things they never imagined they would be used for – for example through the fog of banter and badinage it has dimly come to the attention of the poor our fellas that some of the modern lads have been known to shave the hair on their chest because . . . because . . . well, at that point, again it just gets away from them.

A poor ould fella could be sitting there for a thousand years thinking deeply about why a man would want to shave the hair on his chest in order to make himself feel better about who he is and about life in general, and still no answer would come. If the shaving is not being done in a hospital for an operation, the poor ould fella will not understand it, any part of it.

He hears too that there are men who shave the hair under their arms, again for reasons of personal fulfilment, and he is utterly unable to come to terms with this. But he imagines that if the social worker dropped in on him unexpectedly and he just happened to be shaving off the hair on his chest or under his arms, a few minutes later he would hear the sound of a siren and of a large van pulling up outside, to take him away. And he would ask no questions.

No, in characteristic fashion, he would go quietly.

Even More Bullshit . . .

TED Talks
Motivational speaking
Photographs of farmers on crisp packets
Interpretive centres
Arts festivals
Music festivals
Food festivals
All festivals
Athletics
Swimming
Nature walks
Fancy coffees
Executive airport lounges
IKEA
Bus and taxi lanes
Newgrange
Electric cars
Cremation

Apparently in Dublin there's a bus that goes to IKEA

Not a Good Look

The poor ould fellas, you may have noticed, do not have beards.

On reflection, this may be seen as unusual, as they are not required to attend many public functions and therefore they would be free to 'let themselves go' on the beard front if they so desired.

Nor are they frequently invited onto TV programmes such as *Dancing with the Stars*, where their appearance might be monitored by a large viewing audience nor are they indeed invited onto anything of any kind – their time is their own, as they say.

So there is really nothing stopping them growing a beard of the most extravagant length, though 'growing' is probably not the right word, it seems too 'proactive' – they would simply not bother shaving any more, and let it grow.

And yet a poor ould fella has never grown a beard or let one grow or any combination thereof. You will not see him basing his 'look' on that of the French footballer Olivier Giroud, whose beard is so beautifully cultivated he has been criticised for devoting too much attention to his beardedness and not enough to the task of sticking the ball in the back of the net for Arsenal and now Chelsea.

No, you will not find a poor ould fella being so accused – he will receive many forms of insult or abuse, inflicted consciously or unconsciously, but at least he will never be condemned for having spent too much time taking care of his beard and not enough working. For him that would not be a good look.

He is lacking some essential vanity that would persuade him to stop scraping the ould razor across his face and start experimenting with the 'smig', as country people call it. That hipster look is not for him. There is no image in our minds of a poor ould fella thoughtfully stroking his bearded chin, musing on some esoteric matter of culture or society, and certainly none of him spinning a choice vinyl cut on a Dansette in a continental-style Dublin coffee bar.

Indeed that whole concept of listening to records as a form of entertainment, at home or in a busy café, is one to which the poor ould fellas are total strangers. They just missed out on that one, as they missed out on so many of life's small pleasures.

These men have no record collections. If ever you

enter the abode of a poor ould fella, you can be sure that you will see no shelves filled with LPs, you will not find him flicking through his albums, agonising over whether to play a few tracks off the Yes triple album *Tales From Topographic Oceans* or maybe something raunchier, a side of *Heat Treatment* by Graham Parker & The Rumour or perhaps something from the classic Andy Warhol 'banana' album by The Velvet Underground & Nico.

Though they have a keen sense of loss in their lives, with much justification, at least they do not mourn the death of vinyl or pine for the crackle of a proper twelve inch album. They will not be joining with other poor ould fellas in bemoaning the inferior sound of a CD compared to a 'real' record, nor will they be pounding the table in the cosy bar, giving out about the great art form that was the twelve inch album sleeve and what a swizz the shrunken CD cover is by comparison – no, such changes for the worse in popular culture do not get them going. They can live with the disappearance from our lives of the groundbreaking work of the Hipgnosis design team, they will not be arguing long into the night about the relative merits of those classic sleeves that Hipgnosis did for the Floyd and Wishbone Ash – no, that is not the hill on which the poor ould fellas would want to die.

You may be sure that there are other hills on which they will die, whether they like it or not. But they will not be totally fired up about the overall state of the music business in these times of Spotify and poor sound quality in general on the internet. And they will most certainly not be complaining about the piracy of music on YouTube and its cynical exploitation of the artist, as they carefully remove another priceless waxing from the turntable and clean off the dust with a carbon fibre LP brush, maintaining their collection in the pristine condition that they demand – partly because, as we explained, they have no collection.

The World of Music

Likes:
Johnny McEvoy

Dislikes
U2
Sinéad O'Connor
Glen Hansard
Hozier
And all other
  modern music

Nor is there an elaborate sound system installed in the living rooms of these impoverished old men, in fact there are no sound systems even of a rudimentary kind. You might even say that there is no living room in the conventional sense of a welcoming environment with an array of creature comforts in which a person might wish to spend some downtime – there is no downtime for the poor ould fellas, there is just time . . . time . . . time.

So if you are passing the house of such a man, you will almost certainly not be hearing from within the sounds of a live album on which the crowd is cheering wildly as the main man declares: 'On your feet or on your knees, it's the Blue . . . Oyster . . . Cult!'

That would not be their way.

They missed out on this idea of music as a form of home entertainment, indeed they missed out on just about everything that could be called entertainment, be it home or away. Again it speaks to the spartan nature of their existence, the spurning of life's vanities.

So yes in theory they could be there, lounging in an easy chair, carefully trimming their freshly shampooed beards, playing the imaginary drums along with Derek and the Dominos . . . in theory, if you are theorising about something that could never possibly happen in fifty billion years.

But in truth, you will not encounter such a vision, because such things are for others, not for the poor ould fellas. Scenes that would appear mundane in the lives of other folks seem impossibly exotic when we try to place the poor ould fellas in them, in the mind's eye.

Therefore, you will not find them joining a gym. Even in the unlikely event of them deciding that they need to get themselves 'into shape', they will not be putting themselves down for membership of a gym in the nearest town, to which they might well have to cycle anyway – which would mean they'd already be 'in shape' to all intents and purposes, by the time they get there.

Yes, life itself has done much to get them 'into shape', and to keep them that way, as they traverse the lonely hills at night in the snow, to save the few sheep that are out there, leading their own bleak existence.

So you will never find a poor ould fella who is overweight, nor will you find one who looks at himself in the mirror one day and decides that he needs a bit more muscle-tone, a bit more . . . definition on the 'abs'.

The poor ould fellas have no 'abs', or at least they

do not acknowledge that there are such things. Unlike other men, they do not seek the coveted 'six-pack', indeed they hear these distant conversations on the radio in which cheerful young men are engaging in banter about their 'six-pack', and they haven't a fucking clue what they're on about.

They know instinctively that they can't be talking about a six-pack in the true sense – the Guinness sense – so they just assume that this is another area in which the modern lads have raced ahead of them to some far more pleasant land.

No, they have many things to be bothering them, to be keeping them from their rest, but for the poor ould fellas, worrying about the money they are spending on a gym membership that they hardly ever use will never be a problem.

They are spared that one, at least.

The time has gone, too, when they will be fretting about the differences between the 'traditional' porter that they have enjoyed, and these 'craft beers' that they hear so much about – albeit in that same distant way that they hear about abs and six-packs and all that stuff.

The craft beers, they are hearing, are much better for you than the old-style beers because they have fewer chemicals in them, or something. Though for this you will pay 'a premium', which to the poor ould fellas sounds like something that they do not have.

Nor would they greatly relish the prospect of change of any kind but particularly the kind of change that would involve them drinking something that isn't porter. I think we can safely say that no poor ould fella will be sitting in the cosy bar, thinking it's about time he broke out of his conservative habits and embraced this new phenomenon of the craft beers.

It is far more likely that after a few glasses of the finest porter he will hear some of the modern lads ordering their craft beers and an amusing thought will form in his ould head and he will say to himself, with a faint smile, 'Craft beers . . . craft beers my hole.'

Holidays in Hell

The poor ould fellas never go on holidays.

Certainly they never go on holidays in the sense that any other person would understand the concept – for example, they never go to a foreign country for a week or ten days of 'sun, sea, and sangria'. No, the sun is not for them, the sea is not for them, the sangria is not for them – even if they knew what sangria was, it still would not be for them.

Nor will you find them settling down after their day's labours, kicking off their shoes and chilling out with a bit of a browse through the special offers available in various Irish country house hotels. Yes, it will be rare poor ould fella who will be thinking, *What I need right now is just a midweek break at Bellinter House or Tinakilly House or Rathsallagh House or any other house.* He will not be getting excited about the prospect of a romantic weekend away in Ballymaloe, with fine dining experiences at every turn, for reasons that are so obvious it would be indecent to enumerate them.

In fact it will not just be a rare poor ould fella who

will be seeking these entertainments, it will be no poor ould fella at all.

Moreover, as you are availing of the splendid facilities at the famed Monart Spa in County Wexford would you at any stage expect to see what can only be described as a poor ould fella sitting there in the sauna in his towelling robe with all his bodily fluids pouring out of him, leaving just a kind of a human shell with a cap on top of it? Or would he be attempting laps of the pool or receiving one of the many 'treatments' from the highly trained massage therapists? No, that would not be an everyday scene at Monart, or indeed an anyday scene in one of these fine emporia that are dedicated to the cleansing and renewal of the mind, the body and the spirit.

And if you ever find yourself taking a family holiday on the Wild Atlantic Way, you may be sure you will not be encountering any cyclists dressed in the traditional costume of the poor ould fellas, getting away from it all.

Indeed the poor ould fellas would regard NOT going on a holiday of any kind as the nearest thing they will ever know to this notion of 'getting away from it all'. When they see an ad on the telly which features loads of delighted people splashing around in a hotel swimming pool in some holiday complex under a beautiful blue sky in Majorca, their only thought is, *Thank God . . . I never had to do that . . . and thank God I never will.*

For them this is not a holiday complex, it is just a complex holiday – far, far too complex to be even trying to imagine it in their poor ould heads. All they can see are trials and embarrassments, no doubt some terrible ordeal at the airport during which they will be seized and interrogated by angry policemen about their passport which is not in order or some such bullshit. And then all the wrong turns they would take at the other end after another grilling from the foreign police. And this is before they even get out of the airports.

The hot weather is utterly unsuitable for men who know only one form of clothing, which is mainly black and thus a bit on the dark side for 'fun' activities such as sunbathing or just hanging out at the poolside bar. Nor will they be first on the floor at the disco, when the disc jockey calls on the crowd to do the Macarena. No, when a poor ould fella is looking at a sunshine holiday brochure, he is looking at a vision of hell.

Though of course there may be moves afoot in the Department of Pretending to Care About the

Poor Ould Fellas to make them go to such places, to put them through yet one more humiliation on life's apparently endless journey.

Yes, you can see the bright young people in the department thinking that the poor ould fellas just need a bit of a break from the monotony, they just need to 'recharge their batteries' by letting themselves go for a while in some sunny place, just to 'get away' as they say.

'Paddy, do you ever manage to get away at all?', you can hear them say when they call in to a poor ould fella to check if he has died yet. You see, those lads live in a world in which people are almost constantly

'away', in which they are always sending emails to fellow professionals and receiving the response that he or she is 'away' until next Tuesday week, and then by the time they have come back, the person who sent the email to them is now 'away', and will be until next Thursday fortnight, by which time . . .

You can see that not much gets done in that world, particularly in relation to looking after the poor ould fellas, many of whom are quite unlikely to be around until next Tuesday week, while next Thursday fortnight is really stretching it.

As for themselves, the poor ould fellas are indeed never 'away'. Though in an odd sense they are 'away' from those who are usually 'away', and that is a kind of a release in itself. That is a kind of permanent holiday, that the poor ould fellas are on, a holiday from those who think holidays are a brilliant idea.

But they do stir out of the old homestead now and again, for the more traditional kind of break, a seat in a car perhaps that would take them to the Galway Races and back again straight after the races of course, just in case anyone wants to drag them into the maelstrom of 'fun' that is Galway on race night – no, that would not be fun for them, that would be whatever is the opposite of fun.

And of course while there are many essentially shallow people who would claim that the poor ould fellas are 'their own worst enemies' here, that everybody needs to 'get away', and that by rejecting the concept of the holiday they are refusing to 'leave their comfort zone', in truth it is the poor ould fellas who are showing the deeper understanding of the meaning of life here.

They do not believe that going to Torremolinos for a week can change any meaningful aspect of the human condition, and particularly the condition in which they routinely find themselves – indeed it is far better to decline such a holiday experience than to get a glimpse of some better place to which they can never belong. In the meantime, they will not be joining with the multitudes in this delusion that a swift sampling of another culture in some way enriches us – since said multitudes will be spending the best parts of their holiday in the Shamrock Lounge anyway, drinking fantastic quantities of Guinness and singing 'The Fields Of Athenry'; not only will they not be imbibing another culture, they will be infecting that culture with the worst of their own.

Intuitively, the poor ould fellas see this as clearly as the TV presenter and polymath Dr Jonathan Miller saw it, when he opined that such holidays were not for him (or for any intelligent person, he implied), that ideally he would move to the house across the road from his own for a week or two, just to gain a different perspective on his existence. This would be quite close to the thinking of the poor ould fellas on this matter, without the part about moving to the house across the road. Or at least it would be their thinking if they felt there was any need to be thinking such obvious things.

As for the 'comfort zone' that they are allegedly refusing to leave, perhaps the only reasonable response is to say, 'Some fucking comfort zone.'

Yes, you'll have the odd poor ould fella who is so unfortunate, he actually finds himself in a room opposite some kind of a psychiatrist, who at some point of the proceedings will put it to him that his lack of experience of other ways of life, other customs and modes of recreation is keeping him in this 'comfort zone'. Which he needs to get out of, to become involved in more 'challenging' situations. To 'bring him out of himself', as they say.

Well, now . . .

In describing the conditions in which the poor ould fellas live and the overall shape of their lives, for some reason we have never been tempted to use the words 'comfort zone'. Just something about that . . . can't quite put a finger on it, but something . . . doesn't ring 100 per cent true with us.

Don't know what it is . . . maybe it's the complete and utter lack of comfort in which they live, in every conceivable sense? Could that be it? Would we be getting warm there?

And as for 'challenging' situations, we presume that the highly paid head-shrinker in question has never himself been 'challenged' by his door being broken down at four in the morning by men who are well aware that there is no other door in these parts for about twelve miles? Certainly they are in their comfort zone when they come calling like this on the poor ould fellas, but that would be the full extent of the comfort on offer on such occasions.

Meanwhile, it is a mark of that superior wisdom of the poor ould fellas to which we alluded that it doesn't take as much to 'bring them out of themselves' as it would take many of the rest of us.

Mostly they prefer to keep themselves to themselves anyway, but if there's any 'bringing out' to be done, it doesn't take two weeks in Benidorm, drinking and fornicating, to do it for them. In certain parts of the country at least, all it takes is a wee trip to some nearby town on the Fifteenth of August. A poor ould fella living in an isolated part of County Monaghan, for example, might receive a lift to the seaside village of Blackrock, County Louth, on 'the Fifteenth' and there he would sit against the windowsill of one of the pubs for a while, having an ould smoke, watching the rest of the people enjoying themselves on this strangely festive day in that region, but mainly waiting for the pub to open.

At which point he would repair inside to consume a few glasses of stout, happy to be hearing the sounds from outside, whatever they are, without any need to be participating, as such.

And then he would go home.

To his 'comfort zone'.

The Football Man

The case of John Giles tells us a great deal about life in Ireland.

He has been one of the most beloved public figures of the past fifty years, one of the few well-known people who is still trusted by the broad majority of the citizenry, in particular by a certain section of the population who are, shall we say, of limited means, advanced years and of the male gender.

And there are very good reasons why he has been so loved and trusted. For a start, he was very good at something, which is usually not an essential requirement for fame in Ireland, but which is still appreciated by some.

He was very good at the soccer, really very good, as distinct from not really being very good. Indeed he was so good at it, he was one of the best players not just in Ireland, but in Great Britain – you could even say he was one of the best in Europe, one of the best in the world.

And after he stopped playing the soccer, he was also

very good at being a soccer manager, in particular for the Republic of Ireland, which used to organise its affairs in such a way that the team could end up being picked by a committee member whose expertise lay in other areas – before Giles, it was considered not unusual to have a butcher from Sligo or an auctioneer from Moate selecting the first eleven.

So that's two things he was very good at – three things, actually, when you consider that we haven't even mentioned his television career yet and the fact that as a member of the RTÉ panel he educated a few generations about the game, establishing himself in the process as a television personality of the highest stature. In this respect one might compare him to David Attenborough, though Attenborough's greatest achievement was obviously the creation of *Match of the Day*, whereas Giles actually played in games shown on *Match of the Day*, many times.

Moreover, he was very good at these three things without ever displaying even the slightest trace of eejitry, a trait that was once thought essential for success in public life in Ireland. Which makes it four things he was very good at, five if you include the fact that not only did he not do eejitry, he did an important service to the community by using the proceeds of his massively bestselling autobiography *A Football Man* to start the John Giles Foundation for the benefit of young soccer players in deprived areas.

And then there was a sixth thing that he was very good at, a thing that should be seen as the greatest gift of the many he bestowed on the people of Ireland – over the years, speaking his truth and his wisdom on the TV, before and after the soccer matches, he brought a kind of peace to the lives of the poor ould fellas.

Peace . . . such a precious thing, yet so elusive for the poor ould fellas, who find that the universe has been constructed with the sole purpose of ensuring that everything brings them the opposite of peace. Everything is organised in such a way that they know no ease, no relaxation.

Indeed even on those rare occasions when somehow they find a fleeting moment of relaxation, invariably they encounter something that screams to them in strident tones, 'Stop relaxing . . . stop relaxing . . . stop relaxing . . . stop relaxing!'

Only when John Giles was on the RTÉ Television did they ever truly relax in their own homes – or any other home.

Only when he was speaking in ways that were so wondrously free of bullshit could they find this release from the constant strain of living in a 'stop-relaxing' environment. Indeed it was only in these moments of true relaxation that they fully understood just how unrelaxed they are the rest of the time.

As Gilesy put forward his views on the day's play, in that calm and measured and pragmatic way of his, for the poor ould fellas it was as if they had partaken of the finest opium. His refusal to indulge in attention-seeking antics, coupled with the deep intelligence and essential dignity that emanated from every pore of his being made them wonder how he was ever asked on television in the first place. Indeed if there was ever a scintilla of unease that disturbed their otherwise perfect relaxation, it was the vague fear that some day this would be taken away from them, that some day some clown might realise that a terrible mistake had been made, that Gilesy should never have been there in the first place and was now being assigned to other RTÉ duties which did not involve appearing on television.

And yet they did not worry too much about this, because there seemed to be this sense of true permanence in the presence of John Giles, who had been an important figure in Irish life since the 1960s and who was now in that rarefied category of people who seem to have transcended this mortal realm, with a plaque being erected to mark his birthplace in Ormond Square and his receiving of the Freedom of Dublin.

No, the poor ould fellas thought to themselves, they will not be getting rid of Gilesy now. We can relax.

Turns out they relaxed too soon. Turns out that in one of the most spectacularly cretinous decisions ever made by a television station, RTÉ decided that at the age of seventy-five, John Giles would now be 'retired'.

Why?

Well . . . because he was . . . like . . . seventy-five.

Now the poor ould fellas are not unreasonable men, and they realise that being seventy-five can sometimes make you a bit unsure of your footing in various ways, literal and metaphorical, that it can dim the faculties of even the most clear-headed of commentators. But there was nothing wrong with Gilesy, not one thing. Indeed it is obvious from his continuing appearances on Newstalk Radio that not only was there nothing wrong with him, he was still more right about most things than any other human being in Ireland, and possibly on this earth.

But they 'retired' him anyway from the panel, which not only obliterated one of the few forms of relaxation the poor ould fellas had ever known, it also gave them this message: if we can do this to a seventy-five-year-old man who is functioning at a very high level and who shows no signs of deterioration of his considerable powers, just think what we can do to you, old-timer, you who are already half-dead and who weren't very alive in the first place anyway.

Naturally it did not occur to RTÉ executives that their asinine decision might cause unhappiness among the poor ould fellas because, as we know, the happiness or unhappiness of poor ould fellas is regarded by key decision-makers as being in roughly the same category as the well-being or otherwise of the African dung beetle.

Nor did commentators rush to point out an anomaly here, that in these times of enlightenment in the workplace, in which people are supposed to have certain human rights, you're just not supposed to get rid of people 'because they're seventy-five', no more than you can get rid of someone 'because he's thirty-five'. And when it was suggested that RTÉ was now looking to the future and the long-term development of other panellists, at no point did anyone point out that for certain viewers of a particular demographic there is no future, or at least not much. There is no long-term, there isn't even much of a short-term.

They will just not be there to witness the day when one of the modern lads becomes as good as Gilesy. But then no viewer of any age should have to wait that long for anything.

Imagine, then, the desolation of the poor ould fellas as they realised that the source of their relaxation had been turned into yet another source of agitation. Some of them still refuse to believe it, they sit there looking at a modern lad, thinking that he must be doing a kind of an RTÉ training programme, that he'll get up and leave soon and let old Gilesy take it from there.

But some of them know that it is all true, that they really have sustained this terrible blow, and that there's nothing they can do about it because, if there was, that too would be 'discontinued', as they say.

What relaxation is left to them now, in this post-Giles TV world?

Well, while other people may enjoy various nature programmes, with soothing pictures of rivers and lakes, the poor ould fellas are more concerned with pictures of flooding on the RTÉ news, because there's a certain part of the country that is more vulnerable to flooding than other parts – it doesn't have a geographical name, as such, you could simply call it 'wherever-the-poor-ould-fellas-live'.

So they sit there, looking at the flooding on the news, wondering when the water is going to come lapping through the front door. And that's about as relaxing as it gets for them.

It might be different if RTÉ's Mary Kennedy was the first reporter sailing up to the house in a canoe and coming through the door in her waders, to inspect the damage and to ask them if they're insured, which of course they're not. But it won't be Mary Kennedy, that would be too much to expect. It will be somebody who is in all likelihood much younger than Mary Kennedy and not as friendly.

But maybe Mary Kennedy will come down to them in a few months' time for *Nationwide*, to look back on how the flooding ruined their lives and to pretend that they've pulled themselves together again, to pretend that they're looking to a brighter future.

At least they feel that Mary Kennedy will be around for some time to come, that they won't wake up one day to discover that Mary too has been 'retired' and that *Nationwide* is now being presented by Hector, because he has more 'jizz' in him.

Yes, they feel that Mary is safe enough for a while anyway but, after Gilesy, they do not feel this with any confidence. They do not feel anything with any confidence, they are just hoping.

Hoping against hope.

The World of TV Compères

Likes:
Marty Whelan
Mary Kennedy
Anne Cassin
Ray D'Arcy
David Attenborough
Eileen Dunne

Dislikes:
Ryan Tubridy

The End of the Analog

One day the poor ould fellas found out that their lives were about to be made just a little bit more complicated. This was not an unusual event in itself, as there is clearly a whole branch of the Irish public service that is focused on the invention of ways to diminish whatever small pleasure these men derive from their existence, with a view to extinguishing it altogether going forward.

But this one was particularly dispiriting, because not only did it require them to make some change to their way of life – and change, as we have demonstrated, is not their strong suit – the instructions for this change seemed to be arriving in a language that to them was incomprehensible.

It had words like 'analog' and 'digital', it was talking about something called 'Saorview', it referred to things such as a 'set-top box'. And it was implied in these announcements, which were frequently broadcast on RTÉ, that if the poor ould fellas couldn't figure out what the fuck they were on about, the television screen on which they watched the few programmes they enjoyed would soon have nothing on it. Nothing at all.

Which would probably not stop the poor ould fellas from looking at it anyway for a few hours a day, staring into the void of the blank screen, hoping against hope for some flicker of life, some signal however weak, from within the unresponsive machine. Hoping against hope, but knowing deep down that there would be no deliverance from this emptiness, from this insuperable deadness.

Not an unfamiliar feeling for them, it must be said, though they would be particularly despondent at the loss of the poor ould telly, not because of the programmes, which of course are mostly shit, but because the light and the sound and even the small bit of heat coming out of it kind of keeps them company. Jack the dog also finds it soothing in some strange way known only to himself to be just sitting there with his master looking at the news. And when a wildlife programme comes on, Jack might start yelping when he hears some animal noise which to him is meaningful.

So it is roughly the same experience, then, for man and dog, but it took that ominous turn when they started hearing these announcements by RTÉ that they were switching off this 'analog' signal, that it would be all

'digital' or 'Saorview' or some such fucking nonsense, which according to the experts would mean that from now on there would be good reception all the time.

That in itself was something of a disappointment to the poor ould fellas, who had experienced such bad reception over the years, for reasons that escaped them, that they had just started to get used to it and even to enjoy it. Now they were starting to get the message that this would be the end of the bad reception, there would either be crystal clear reception or no reception at all.

Which was it to be? The announcement seemed to contain an unspoken threat, that the days of sticking an aerial on top of the television were gone, that at some point in what was bound to be a harrowing journey the poor ould fellas would need this thing called a 'set-top box'. And if they couldn't tune that in themselves – not a very big 'if' there – in the mind's eye they could see themselves needing to employ the services of a TV repairman to do the tuning. A man who would arrive in a van, a man to whom they would have to listen as he talked gibberish to them in a Dublin accent, a man to whom they would have to give money.

Mind you, they had heard that the good reception, this 'high definition' thing, is so clear it is like putting on a pair of glasses, and then putting another pair of glasses on top of them, for extra clarity. That it would probably be good for watching hurling matches, what with the small ball, or at least the hurling matches that the GAA hasn't already sold off to Sky.

Here was another issue to be troubling them on top of the great 'analog' crisis, which was eventually solved for many of them by the district nurse explaining it properly and just making whatever minor adjustments needed to be made, without having to call in the man with the van from Dublin.

No, the selling of the rights of Gaelic games to Sky was truly beyond their control, a cultural atrocity committed without the slightest concern for the needs and wishes of that sector of the community that was most vulnerable to change in this regard, a sector that comprises those who are poor, those who are ould and those who are fellas.

It is not really an 'option' for such men to be trying to watch these games on 'the big screen' in 'a sports bar', they are just not happy in themselves in that atmosphere. And anyway they had assumed that even if no enjoyment of any other kind was to come their way in this last unremittingly dreary episode of their lives, they would at least be able to turn on the telly and watch the big Gaelic match on RTÉ.

Now even that has been taken from them. Now RTÉ, the station they have, is showing some but not all of the big games, and some but not all of the small games too. And Sky, the station they don't have, is showing the rest.

In return for Rupert Murdoch's money, the GAA has decided that it is acceptable to lower the already low quality of life of some of their most loyal adherents, some of the men who made the GAA what it is today, and whore themselves for the Australian's dollar, indifferent to the desires of their true supporters.

Ah, it is very sad. And of course there is no other

The World of Sport

Likes:
Ted Walsh
Ruby Walsh
Katie Walsh
Lionel Messi
Mick O'Dwyer
John Giles
Pádraig Harrington

Dislikes:
Conor McGregor
Cristiano Ronaldo
José Mourinho
Lance Armstrong
Wayne Rooney
Jim Gavin
Stephen Cluxton

'option' for the poor ould fellas in terms of 'streaming' or any of those other tricks that the modern lads can do on the internet to watch football matches. Indeed they were just thinking of getting a video recorder – because they'd heard that you could watch these 'videos' of old football matches – when the video recorder was abolished.

Gone are the days too when TG4 would show *All-Ireland Gold*, with maybe the 1961 football final or the 1967 Railway Cup matches, which was always a treat for the poor ould fellas, because to them they were like 'live' matches. By some quirk of the ageing process they had once known the results of these games, and known them very well, but that knowledge had now

completely disappeared from their heads, so that they would be coming to these encounters with a clean slate, as it were. An open mind – if by 'open' here we mean a mind from which most important information has been erased – the advantage of which was that they could now be watching a 'recording' of an All-Ireland final as if it was happening here and now.

Certainly it is rare for the poor ould fellas to have an advantage over any other human being in any field of endeavour, and in this case in order to get it, first they had to be disadvantaged in every other way. And now that they don't show *All-Ireland Gold* any more, society doesn't have to worry about that particular injustice, doesn't have to be fretting that the poor ould fellas might be getting one up on them there.

As for other viewing 'options', there will be no Netflix in the world of the poor ould fellas, and if you were to call on one of them unannounced, it is most unlikely that you will find him binge-watching a boxset. Indeed sometimes these days you will hear affluent young people complaining that their leisure hours are being consumed by this compulsion that they have, this addiction to binge-watching boxsets – this is one bullet at least that the poor ould fellas have dodged.

Still, they live with this anxiety that due to circumstances beyond their control, the celebrity architect Dermot Bannon will come to their poor ould house some day to do his hit RTÉ programme *Room to Improve*, and he will start changing everything. Such is their anxiety about this, that he starts to haunt their dreams, does Bannon, knocking down the walls to create more space, always more space, so much fucking space he seems to think that poor ould fellas are in the habit of entertaining large numbers of guests at their famous soirees, or that they love to have a few people around in the morning for a bit of a gossip around the breakfast bar – for which purpose Bannon will be bulldozing whatever is there and putting in said breakfast bar. Whether the poor ould fella likes it or not, which of course he does not.

Then he wakes up from this dream, and for a moment the poor ould fella is almost happy that his life is the way it is, and not the way Dermot Bannon wants it to be.

Almost . . . almost happy.

But not quite.

The World of Celebrities

Likes:
Barack Obama
Marty Whelan
Mary Kennedy

Dislikes:
Harvey Weinstein
Johnny Depp
Jeremy Clarkson
And all other celebrities

ILLNESS,
INFIRMITY AND
EXTINCTION

Waiting for the Operation

At any given time, a poor ould fella will be in need of some kind of operation. He will hear it called a 'procedure' by the medics but to him it will always be an operation, and it will always take a lot longer to be performed than would be 'optimal', as the lads in the white coats might put it.

This is due to a number of factors, chief among them being that nobody gives a damn whether a poor ould fella has his operation or not. On the whole there is a quiet consensus that they would all be better off just dying en masse if possible, thus freeing up the overburdened health service for the treatment of more urgent cases – indeed there is an unspoken ratings system in place, whereby the ingrown toenail of the prosperous country solicitor is prioritised over the late-stage lung cancer of the poor ould fella, and nobody feels too bad about it.

Of course if they had an expensive health- insurance plan it might be different, but then they would be rich ould fellas, and we are not interested in them.

So they spend their days waiting and waiting and waiting for the operation. Sometimes the waiting goes on for so long, they've actually forgotten what the operation is for, they just know they need to have something taken out of them or at least that they should have had this done maybe a couple of years ago.

They have spent so much time in doctors' waiting rooms they have memorised most of the messages on the noticeboard – which is quite a thing really when you consider they are no longer able to remember the detail of almost anything that happened to them since, say, 1961. Other than a general sense that it probably wasn't much good.

When they first saw some information about holistic healing, as they waited for another hour after the two hours they'd already been waiting to see the doctor, they had no idea what holistic healing might be. But they have been looking at the leaflet about it for so long now that they're starting to form a rough idea of what it is and why it wouldn't be right for them.

Likewise they are all-too-familiar with the cards

bearing the names of counsellors and psychotherapists, who seem to be providing some sort of a service to the rest of the general public but who are quite intimidating to the poor ould fellas. The idea that they would be talking about themselves to a total stranger for the best part of an hour about their feelings – whatever the hell they are – is a somewhat alien one.

The main feeling they have is that they wouldn't want to do that. In fact the feeling that they really don't want to talk about their feelings may be one of the strongest feelings they have ever had. In the mind's eye, the most they could see themselves doing in the way of this 'therapy' is sitting down for an hour in total silence, waiting for the counsellor to tell them what is wrong with them and when they're supposed to be having the operation.

But they suspect that that's not how it works. They are probably still more comfortable with the older style of confessional healing, whereby you went to Confession, kneeling in a dark booth babbling about your 'sins' while a deeply unhappy man sat on the other side of the grille, listening to this shit and imposing some form of penance – the talking therapy that they call 'prayer'.

It was a system that suited a certain type of person, not least the older male members of the community, who would be far more reluctant to be revealing their sins to someone sitting across a table from them in broad daylight, someone much younger than them who is more than likely not a priest and who wants them to embark on a process of change.

The man on the other side of the grille didn't want them to change, in fact it suited everyone that they would say the few prayers he gave them for penance, sure in the knowledge that they'd be back again in a few weeks with exactly the same things to 'confess', and so the great wheel of life would turn.

Change was not on the menu, because all parties to the process believed that change is bad – all change, all the time, is bad. And while some would dismiss this as a 'negative' response, there is quite a compelling reason why the poor ould fellas might regard change as a bad thing, that reason being that it has totally destroyed every aspect of their lives.

And it has done so systematically, relentlessly, comprehensively. It has done so to such an extent, there is no therapy that could put it right, except to stop it all, to put an end to all change, immediately. And then to reverse all the changes that have already been made.

Anyway, the only 'therapy' they need, the only 'breakthrough' they'd be looking for, is to turn on the telly one day and see that RTÉ is showing an old episode of *The Virginian* instead of repeats of the previous night's episodes of *Home and Away*, *Neighbours*, *EastEnders* and *Fair City* – which they avoided the first time due to the correct supposition on their part that they are not exactly the demographic the makers of these shows are trying to reach.

Indeed nobody who makes anything for public consumption is trying to reach them, if truth be told. But it is particularly obvious that they would not be uppermost in the thoughts of the makers of a show such as *EastEnders*. No, when a poor ould fella tries to settle his poor ould bones into the couch for the evening, we can safely say that he won't be sitting there in anticipation of the latest doings of various psychotic Londoners with their shouting and their roaring. That he won't be miming the dramatic drumbeats at the start of each episode or savouring the same music at the end as the credits roll, trying to time his imaginary drumming so that he nails it exactly on the opening beat – no, he won't be doing any of that.

He has seen people like this before on *The Jeremy Kyle Show*, which he would sometimes watch by mistake in the mornings on TV3. 'If I'm not your father then you're married to your brother!' might be the topic of the day or 'You agreed to meet me for sex when you thought I was another woman!' or maybe 'My lesbian niece doesn't know if her gay ex-boyfriend is the father!'

Clearly a poor ould fella might not instantly identify with these themes nor with the, shall we say, uninhibited personalities of the protagonists. So the kind of change he would be looking for in his own life would be to change *The Jeremy Kyle Show* from one that is made and then shown on the telly to one that is not made and therefore does not exist in any form.

Yes, if the people who thought of such shows could just go back to where they were before they thought of it and change what they did next, so that they didn't do *The Jeremy Kyle Show* at all, that is the kind of change the poor ould fellas could get behind – to change whatever changes have been made, that would be ideal.

But that is not the kind of change that the medics

and those in the caring professions in general are offering them. So they wait and they wait, in all those waiting rooms, staring at information about reflexology and Pilates – the medics are always talking about the Pilates, and how it would be great for the ould back, and how, even though they might have to join a class full of women doing physical jerks, it would be worth it, because it strengthens your core. The poor ould fellas feel that they'd be spoiling the show by explaining that they no longer have a core.

They have become aware of the concept of preventative medicine in their reading of the 'literature', though they realise that the only kind of preventative medicine that had a chance of working was for them not to be born at all. And as for aromatherapy, this too would be of limited value to men whose ailments are at an advanced stage – and who have been known themselves to give off aromas that are complex, challenging and even overpowering.

But there is one new finding in the area of diet and nutrition that brings a wintry smile to their lips. Mostly they can ignore the advice about not eating rich food – they don't have the money for it – and not eating processed food such as Galtee cheese and Knorr soup, because the damage is already done there.

But Guinness has always contained certain nutrients, it is 'good for you' as part of a balanced diet – and in Ireland, even as part of an unbalanced diet, it has been proven to sustain human life in the absence of almost any other food or drink. And now there is such a thing as vegan Guinness. Indeed since Diageo removed some sort of dead fish substance from the filtration process, all Guinness products are now suitable for vegans. Which means, as the day of the operation finally draws near and the nerves of the poor ould fellas become even more frayed, they can be said to be totally vegan.

More vegan than the vegans themselves.

The World of Literature

Likes:
Dick Francis
Freddie Forsyth

Dislikes:
Salman Rushdie*
Alexandr Solzhenitsyn*
John Banville*
J.M. Coetzee*
Bill Cullen

*Have never actually read any books
  by these people because they're
  obviously all a cod

The Operation

For anyone about to have an operation, life can get a bit complicated. But they tend to have what is called a 'support system' in place, a modern term which means that someone, somewhere, gives a fuck.

The same could not be said for the poor ould fellas. Though since they are accustomed to this state of being and have absolutely no expectations of anything else, that is the least of their troubles as the ambulance pulls up outside the door to take them away on this latest adventure.

Indeed it hardly even strikes them as odd that Jack the dog has more of a 'support system' than they have because at least some other poor ould fella who lives in the next house seven miles away has agreed to take Jack for the week – though in the ultimate act of loyalty, Jack has been feeling poorly too, and so it may fall to the poor ould fella who is taking him to arrange to have him humanely destroyed in the not entirely unlikely event that his ailing master does not come home.

At the hospital they will be confronted with oddness at every turn – things that are odd to them, at least, which may not seem odd to modern people, such as the lift on the ground floor of the hospital. Certainly there are some poor ould fellas who have been in a lift before but we are personally acquainted with some who have not had this experience and who may find it disturbing.

We know of one poor ould fella in particular who lives in County Wicklow who had never been in a lift in his life until they installed one in the Bridgewater Shopping Centre in Arklow – he was eighty-one at the time and in what had been a largely agricultural existence, he had somehow missed out on this life experience. Perhaps if he had been in the habit of going to Dublin for the weekend, staying overnight at the Shelbourne Hotel with his partner and taking in a show at the Bord Gáis Theatre, he would not have been lacking this particular knowledge of how the world works – perhaps indeed if he had been in the habit of going on the occasional city break to London or Madrid or Vienna, just grabbing his passport and heading off for a stress-busting weekend to some such destination, he would be as familiar as you or me with the internal mechanics of large modern public buildings.

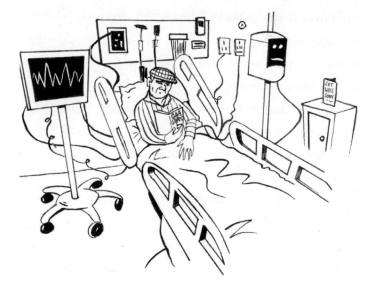

But he was not in these habits, nor would some of his elderly rural brethren be completely untroubled by the challenge of getting from the ground floor to the twelfth floor in the magic moving box – not that anyone else would be aware of this slight complication, because the poor ould fellas do not share their anxieties with others, lest they be mocked.

As it happens, the poor ould fella going in for the operation finds that he quite enjoys the sensation of the hospital lift going up twelve floors so smoothly and so quickly, savouring the thought that for once in his life, he seems to be doing something the easy way. In fact he is finding it hard to suppress an urge to ask the nurse if she would let him go down in the lift and up again just for sport. But suppress it he does, the result of many years of practice in the area of urge-suppression in general.

But no doubt there are other poor ould fellas who would find that first ride in a lift to be most disconcerting. Another issue of this nature arises in the hospital when they are advised by the medics that due to the dangers of superbugs and the like, it is essential that all visits to the bathroom be followed by a thorough washing of hands.

While the poor ould fellas are sure that they will get the superbug anyway, that no amount of handwashing will spare them that inevitable calamity, they will also struggle with an issue that has always affected them in their visits to public toilets in general – when they turn on the tap in the hand basin, they can find no way to turn it off.

They try turning the tap from right to left and from left to right, they press the top of it, they wonder if it will stop of its own accord after a while, and so they wait for that to happen, but it doesn't.

They know there is a knack to it, and that they don't have that knack – so they can only hope there is nobody else there to witness their inadequacy or to report them to the authorities if, as seems likely to them, they have started a process which will lead to the flooding of the entire building and its evacuation.

There's another knack they don't have, the knack of using the automatic hand-dryer, which can defeat them in a variety of ways – they may be looking for a

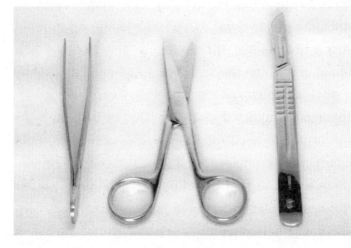

button on it, which it doesn't have, or they may think that they only have to put their hands under it for the heat to start blowing, when in fact they need to press a button. And if they find themselves trying to use one of the advanced Dyson machines, usually they need to wait to observe some modern person using it. By which time their hands are dry anyway.

In fact it will have taken them so long to get the tap

to stop running, there wouldn't be much drying left in the first place.

And while these would not seem to be the most pressing problems, given that the poor ould fella is about to undergo some massive operation for reasons that he barely comprehends, still it reminds us that there are features of everyday life that present no difficulty of any kind to the population at large but that can befuddle those already befuddled by just about everything they encounter in the public realm.

For example, when regular folks complain about the agonies inflicted upon them when they have the misfortune to need the services of someone in a call centre, they are unaware that for the poor ould fellas there is one further indignity to be endured – since the best phone they would have is one of the old rotational dial-up variety, when they are instructed by the automatic voice to press button 1, 2, 3, 4, 5, 6, 7, 8 or 9, they must face the maddening reality that they have no such buttons. That they can't even gain entrance to this hell that is open to other people, that they are stuck in some sort of anteroom in which an even more exquisite torment is to be found.

Indeed in much of their dealings with the health service in the weeks and months before the operation, they were frequently being asked to do things that were not within their skill set, such as 'replying to an email' or 'receiving a text confirming the date of the procedure'. To which in an ideal world of the imagination, recognising the absurdity of their being asked to perform an act which to them is so unnatural, they would shoot back a reply such as 'LOL' or 'LMAO' or even 'ROFL'. But then that would require them to know what a text is and what an email is and what LOL and LMAO and ROFL are. And that would take some time.

But at least in the hospital they are given a pair of pyjamas. It is now generally understood even by those at management level in the health service that the kinds of shops to which the poor ould fellas would once have gone for the pyjamas, such as Clerys, no longer exist. And they have yet to become adept at exploring the online options in sourcing night attire because for them the internet does not exist either.

The other patients in the ward by contrast are permanently on their smartphones, which enables them to avoid all meaningful contact with the new arrival in the institutionalised pyjamas. This suits the man in the pyjamas too because he can't think of anything he might say to them in the unlikely event

Ailments They Have

Bronchitis
Lumbago
Alzheimer's
Emphysema
Arthritis
Blood pressure
Bad with their nerves
Pneumonia
Diabetes
Alcoholism
Angina
Ulcers
Lumbago (again)
Cataracts
prostate
Deafness
Blindness
Gallstones
Haemorrhoids
Dizziness
Palpitations
Hodgkin's lymphoma

Non-Hodgkin's
 lymphoma
Frozen shoulder
Cholesterol
Irritable bowel syndrome
Sleep apnoea
Coronary artery disease
Parkinson's
Restless legs syndrome
Rheumatism
Cardiovascular disease
Vertigo
Erectile dysfunction
Goitre
Hypothermia
Kidney stones
Arteriosclerosis
Farmer's lung
Gastroenteritis
Neuropathy
Urinary tract infections
Tinnitus
More lumbago

Ailments They Don't Have

None

When get check for it, they have to stick their finger up

that they might say something to him – which he probably can't hear anyway.

He can tip his cap to them, though, and to the medics who gather around his bed, babbling away to him about the operation, about what they're going to do and for how long they're going to be doing it, displaying all the benefits of the seven years of training it took for them to learn this language known only to themselves. And in a tone that also assures the patient that none of this is any of his business, really, and that any comment he might wish to make on this or any other matter would be superfluous.

He knows only that his ailment has become so advanced, it is too late for a 'keyhole surgery' job, unless the keyhole in question has already been blown open with gelignite. He can vaguely understand it when they say something about him being possibly out of hospital in a week, all things going well 'in theatre', but that it will take another three weeks on top of that when he gets the superbug. (He quietly notes that they did actually say 'when' not 'if'.)

Which sounds fair enough to the poor ould fella, he knows these lads can't work miracles. That would be more in the domain of the 'sad old padre', as Tom Jones might call him, who takes a particular interest in the more elderly patients, because they're the only ones who have a clue what he's doing there, who don't automatically regard him as some kind of a roaming sex predator on day release who has been mysteriously given a licence to engage with the unwell.

The decades of the Rosary that ensue will probably not make much difference to the outcome of the operation. But if they are the last thing the poor ould fella hears on this earth – and they probably will be – he is consoled by the thought that if he ever gets to heaven, it will be a place in which water stops coming out of the tap when you turn the tap off. And where they don't make hot-air dryers that guarantee some sort of public embarrassment for people like him. Or a customer service helpline that can ask you to press a number that is unpressable.

Even in the afterlife, the poor ould fella will not be asking for much. And the smart money says he won't be getting it either.

The sad old padre, striking a note of false optimism, asks him if he has any plans for when he gets out of hospital, which of course he hasn't. There is one thing, though, that he thinks he might like to do, but which he doesn't mention, because it might be bad luck.

He thinks he might like to spend some time just going up and down in the lift. Up and down, up and down.

That's all.

The Last Rites

The wireless is still a source of some small comfort to the poor ould fellas, though they tend to prefer the sort of radio programmes that are not 'interactive', not overly concerned with the views of their listeners. They enjoy that nice John Bowman programme on Sunday mornings on RTÉ, the one in which he goes back to the archives to play bits of interviews with Éamon de Valera or Cardinal Conway or Terry Wogan or perhaps a lovely old song by Margaret Barry or a rousing tune from the Kilfenora Céilí Band. They enjoy it not just because it brings them back to olden days, but because they can be sure that Bowman won't start reading out texts and emails from listeners, that there will be no vox pops.

The poor ould fellas don't like any of that stuff, they would prefer if the presenter waited until the end and then just said something like, 'We asked our listeners what they thought of Donald Trump, and some of them said he was great and some of them said he was a complete cunt.' Or words to that effect.

That would save a lot of time that could better be spent doing the sort of things John Bowman does, like playing excerpts from old programmes about the Kennedy assassination or maybe a funny story about something that happened during the Emergency or, best of all, the voice of Johnny McEvoy singing 'goodbye Muirsheen Durkan sure I'm sick and tired of workin', no more I'll dig the praties, no longer I'll be fooled . . .'

But there aren't many John Bowmans left on the radio, so it can be a tough ask for the poor ould fellas to be listening to programmes that feature about three minutes of the presenter and about three hours of opinions on the great issues of the day offered by the listeners, none of whom seem to be poor ould fellas – who have better things to be doing.

Well, no, that's not true exactly, in the sense that they have nothing at all to be doing. But somehow even doing nothing is better than texting the lad on FM101 to say that you have looked deeply into the issue and you are in favour of a hard Brexit and you want everyone to know it.

Far better to be listening to the local radio station, which is usually a bit more circumspect about reading out every piece of drivel that is sent in to it – local people don't necessarily want other local people to be knowing their business, after all – and for the poor ould fellas there is a special attraction in the item that is usually broadcast at 10 o'clock in the morning during which they read out a list of all the people who have died in the past few days in the locality.

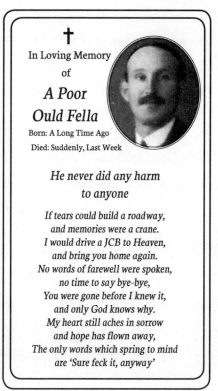

✝

In Loving Memory
of
A Poor
Ould Fella

Born: A Long Time Ago
Died: Suddenly, Last Week

He never did any harm
to anyone

If tears could build a roadway,
and memories were a crane.
I would drive a JCB to Heaven,
and bring you home again.
No words of farewell were spoken,
no time to say bye-bye,
You were gone before I knew it,
and only God knows why.
My heart still aches in sorrow
and hope has flown away,
The only words which spring to mind
are 'Sure feck it, anyway'

Naturally this makes the poor ould fellas feel a little sad, both for the people who have died and because their own names are not on the list. Yes, it would come as a great relief to them to hear that unbeknownst to themselves they have died and will be buried after requiem mass at the Church of the Assumption (a very great Assumption, it must be said) next Tuesday – but they realise that leaving this world will probably be a bit more complicated than that. And staying in it just gets harder by the day.

So they beat on, boats against the current, borne back ceaselessly into the past. As the fellow said.

They light up another smoke and remember all the times they were told that smoking would kill them eventually. And they think, *If only* . . .

Indeed they figure that somehow they've been cheated in this, as in so many other things, that for some perverse reason the cigarette manufacturers have been putting a milder form of poison into their Sweet Aftons than into those smoked by all the faithful departed.

They recall the time the doctor advised them to switch to the vaping. He took out the vaper and he demonstrated how it worked and he recommended it highly – of all the ludicrous propositions that have been put to the poor ould fellas in this general area of health and safety, the suggestion that they should take up the vaping is one that stands out there on its own.

The fucking vaping.

Some fellow with letters after his name actually thought that the day would come when a poor ould fella of his own volition would give up the fags and take up the vaping.

It is not for them.

No, it is not going to happen, this vision of a horde of poor ould fellas vaping away, where once they would be savouring the old Sweet Afton or perhaps the Woodbine. You can't persuade them to choose the inferior method in this, one of the few modest pleasures left to them – doubly pleasing because of the way that it is almost certainly hastening their demise.

In most other parts of their existence they are forced to take the second-best, the third-best, or even the twenty-fourth-best version that is available but, when it comes to smoking, they insist on doing it using cigarettes. And only cigarettes. And the best cigarettes, if possible, the 'best' in this case being the ones that the medics would call the 'worst'.

And yet as they long to find that passage into the next world, in the fervent hope that it bears no resemblance whatsoever to this one, still there are aspects of the death thing that they find problematic.

They have attended too many funerals of late, which are not really funerals at all but cremations. It has got very popular all the same has cremation, but it doesn't sit well with the poor ould fellas. To them a funeral is not really a funeral unless at some point in the proceedings a large box is lowered into a hole in the ground with the dead person inside it.

That is the minimum requirement for them really, anything other than that and they believe they are not really at a funeral but at some sort of Protestant or hippie event, at which people do whatever they want, at which even the dead think they can do things their way and not the way it has been done since time immemorial – the right way, if you like.

The poor ould fellas, you see, have never really been comfortable with this idea of people doing what they want – in any circumstances. They themselves have never done the things they wanted to do and therefore after a while they just stopped wanting things altogether. And even then, though they wanted so little, they found that they wouldn't be getting it anyway. And that there was no point complaining.

So the idea that they could decide to be cremated just because they wanted it seems fundamentally unnatural to them. Since almost everyone they have ever known is dead, they have of course been to many, many funerals, of the traditional variety, but in recent years they have noted this change in the preferred manner of dispatch. They have even been forced to go to Dublin on a few occasions, to the Mount Jerome Crematorium to comply with the last wishes of the deceased to be consigned to the flames, accompanied by the strains of the deceased's favourite song – the poor ould fellas will not be making such a request for their own funeral, regardless of what form it takes. They might have a favourite song but they don't see much point in listening to it when they have been dead for a few days.

Ah, it is all a bit dramatic for them, the cremation, and they are also somewhat fearful that they themselves may somehow end up like this, in an urn, their ashes being scattered over the fucking Ganges or however they do it.

How can they be sure their own wishes will be respected in death, when in life they have been so disregarded? For the powers-that-be, it might be cheaper to burn the poor ould fella than to plant him in the ground where he belongs – he feels that he belongs there anyway, with the sad old padre muttering a few prayers while the gravediggers ease him down into the hole. And maybe Jack the dog would be there too, before he goes to his new home with another poor ould fella a few miles away, himself not long for this world . . .

Indeed perhaps this preference for the grave over the furnace reveals a subconscious desire on the part of the poor ould fella to maintain some connection with Jack, who may be drawn back to this place, to the earth, in a way that he will not be drawn to the Ganges or the Atlantic Ocean or the gust of wind that will take the poor ould fella away, wherever they throw him out of the urn − or maybe they'd just sweep him away into some big heap of ashes containing the cremated remains of all the other poor ould fellas who thought they were getting a proper burial.

He can get a bit down in himself when his mind starts racing like this, so he tries to do what one of the psychiatrists told him and 'focus on the positives' − the main one being that no matter how it turns out, he'll be dead anyway − that is one of the positives. That is a big positive and right now he is struggling to see any negatives there at all.

He can see the simple epitaph, too, on the wooden cross: 'Here lies a poor ould fella. He hated everything about the modern world.'

And you know what?

He was fucking right.

What to Buy Them for Their Birthday

Scratch cards

An online betting voucher (though they haven't got the internet)

200 fags

Six months' subscription to the *Racing Post* (they probably won't last the year)

A tin of Zubes (can be used later as an ashtray)

A pack of cards with pictures of Ireland

Cartridges for a shotgun

Poitín

Nice of her to buy me a scratch card – not that I'll win anything...

What Not to Buy Them for Their Birthday

A ticket to a Conor McGregor fight
  in Las Vegas
Amusing fridge magnets
A voucher for a boutique hotel
The Happy Pear: Recipes for Happiness
Scrabble (nobody to play it with
  anyway)
Nutribullet (for making smoothies)

The Tomb of the Poor Ould Fella

'Nothing is funnier than unhappiness,' said Samuel Beckett and he would know what he was talking about there. He was never one to be shoehorning a happy ending into his books and plays, if it was not appropriate – and it was rarely appropriate, given the themes that the great man favoured.

Our old friend 'isolation' was one of his specialities; a Beckett character tended to be living at a remove from the bourgeois conventions of the age, if living was the right word at all to describe such a bleak existence.

Critics have suggested that the poverty and the general decrepitude of some of the elderly male characters to be found in a Beckett play were directing us towards the broader themes of a decaying civilisation – that these poor unfortunates such as Vladimir and Estragon who have nothing better to be doing except wait for Godot, whoever the fuck he might be, are representative of mankind as a whole in the baleful light of the catastrophes of the twentieth century. They are lost, they are bewildered, they are abandoned in the void.

But then the more we start to think about it, the more it occurs to some of us that, in fact, these characters may not be representative of anything, except perhaps themselves. That when you reflect on the lack of creature comforts in their lives, and their struggles against the onset of various infirmities, on their distinctly male deficiencies, and even on the garb in which they are clothed, what we are looking at, more than anything else, is a bunch of what can only be described as poor ould fellas. When we were watching John Hurt in *Krapp's Last Tape*, what else were we looking at, but a poor ould fella?

Indeed only by realising that Beckett was basically writing about poor ould fellas can we achieve any kind of true understanding of his oeuvre. Know this and you will know much more about the great dramatist and where he was coming from.

And yet you could be listening to the academics blathering about Beckett for the next eight hundred years without one single mention of this obviously powerful source from which he derived so much of his inspiration. They will search for clues in his Irishness in general, without ever alluding to the possibility that

having grown up in a society in which even some of the relatively young fellas could give the impression that they were poor ould fellas, Beckett might have observed some of this, and noted it for future consideration.

When they are assessing the works of John Millington Synge, they are full of enthusiasm about the primitive vitality of the peasants of the West of Ireland, and yet they can be looking at this succession of poor ould fellas being wheeled out by Beckett and all they can talk about are bullshit abstractions such as 'alienation' and 'starkness' and 'post-apocalyptic nothingness'.

Even the corporate bullshitters are taking bits out of Beckett with their wrong-headed adoption of his 'Try again. Fail again. Fail better.' And still nobody seems to have noticed this most important thing about these characters of his – the fact that they have been walking among us all the time, that some of them are still out there and that, even when they have obviously featured in the major works of the greatest playwright of our time, they are utterly ignored.

In just this one narrow sense they would be an invaluable educational resource for students of modern drama. And yet though they still actually look like Beckett characters who have somehow escaped from the theatre into the living world, waiting for something that they know is never going to come, they might as well be invisible.

Nor does the modern world have any use for them and for the wisdom which they may have accrued. Indeed perhaps the cornerstone of that wisdom is the belief that almost everything is bullshit. And it is a belief that is secretly shared by many of the modern lads who would otherwise be mocking the poor ould fellas.

Yes there is an increasing sense that many things have gone wrong in Western society. Even those who have gained much from cultural phenomena such as social media and from the decline of actual culture are suffering in other ways – essentially they are entertaining themselves to death, they are going insane from their incessant consumption of shit, they are aware that almost everything they are doing is wrong.

Well, the poor ould fellas are aware of that too, it's just that they got there a long time before the modern lads and they could have told them about it, if any of them had cared to ask, which of course they didn't.

So at one level the poor ould fellas are greatly to be pitied, for the desolate nature of the universe which they inhabit, yet in some strange way they have achieved a kind of detachment from the world which is greatly to be envied. They have no Fear Of Missing Out – they have already missed out on everything, so they're free from the particular anxiety of FOMO.

Nor do they have the everyday worries of the middle classes – they don't be fretting about what sort of wine to bring along to the dinner party, they don't be tormenting themselves about the amount of time they're spending online and the work/life balance is of no concern to those who have no work or life.

And yet instead of seeing them in a quasi-mystical light, instead of revering them as otherworldly beings, we just pretend they aren't there at all.

Somewhere deep down inside us though, we know that the poor ould fellas can provide us with the seeds of contemplation. In 2018, in Rathdrum, County Wicklow, as part of the county council's town and village renewal scheme, the artist Ellie McNamara was commissioned to create a sculpture in the centre of the town.

She chose to design a piece called 'Fair Day', which has a farmer sitting on a bench with his loyal sheepdog keeping him company. While it may officially be called 'Fair Day', there is no doubt that it must eventually be called the 'Poor Ould Fella'. Because that it who it is.

There he sits, with his poor ould dog, immortalised in bronze. So perfectly does the artist render the essential nature of her subject, it seems like a kind of a national monument to this indigenous people of ours, to this lost tribe.

Indeed in times to come it may be called the 'Tomb of the Unknown Poor Ould Fella' or some such colloquial title which will bespeak its significance. And large numbers of people will come to it, for reasons best known to themselves – perhaps to acknowledge all the poor ould fellas they never knew because they couldn't be bothered. Or because, well, because perhaps there's a little bit of the poor ould fella in all of us.

Already it is a tremendously popular monument, as if it triggers some ancient recognition in the souls of the people. When it is snowing, the poor ould fella and his poor ould dog are given scarves and woolly hats, and it gives them this air of contentment, even a touch of merriment.

You can sit down on the bench beside them, and if you feel like it, you can talk to them. And you don't have to worry – they're not going to ask you for anything.

Frozen forever in the middle of Rathdrum, they are living their best life.

WHAT THE FUTURE HOLDS FOR THE POOR OULD FELLAS

All I ask is that you will remember me at Holy
Communion and on the day of the County Final

JESUS MERCY

MARY HELP

SACRED HEART OF JESUS

Have mercy on the soul of

A POOR OULD FELLA

from a small town in Ireland

Who died last week

Aged over eighty

—R.I.P—

— ✠ —

"He hated everything about the
modern world"

Oh Lord, you have welcomed our beloved, but decrepit, poor ould fella into your Heavenly Paradise. The great consolation which we experience in our unimaginable and incalculable loss is that You have deigned, through obsfuscation, revelation and mystery, to receive him in the bosom of Your almighty merciful palatial paradise of compassion and love. If a plethora of sins holds him captive for a short while in the hot cauldron of despair and unimaginable sufferings , then let our generous prayers offered to You, along with all the beasts and beings incarcerated in the eternal congregation of eternity, heavenly wonders and climate science, bequeath to him, by the unique mercifulness and compassion which has detained him within the confines of you and your Heavenly love, the eternal rest, recuperation, rehabiltation and salvation promised to all of us, in our often tempestuous, but fruitful, relationship with the Almighty, your humble, obedient and worshipful followers who are left here on earth. (God help us.) All our prayers, deeds, sufferings, unpaid holidays, necessary toilings, bountiful meanderings and good works we offer to You so that You may have mercy on our departed soul brother number one whose life was dedicated to the consummate worship and glorification of the eternal truth of God's salvation.

— ✠ —

"Cry 'Havoc!', and let slip the dogs of war".
   Pray for us, O Mother of God,
That we may be at peace,
   And fill our aching hearts with Joy,
And all our shit sufferings cease.
   The vacant gap within our hearts,
We ask you fill with pride,
   "Though they asked for so little
Still it was denied"

The publishers would like to thank the following for use of images:

Dreamstime.com: 16/Captaincoldfront; 30/Creative Commons Zero – publicdomainphotographs; 37/Mikko Pitkänen; 53/Creative Commons Zero – publicdomainstockphotos; 95/Creative Commons Zero – creativecommonsstockphotos; 97/ Creative Commons Zero – creativecommonsstockphotos; 110/Raphotography; 122/Creative Commons Zero – publicdomainstockphotos; 123/Rihardzz; 161/Oded Levran; 170/Creative Commons Zero – creativecommonsstockphotos; 178/Marcus Miranda; 181/Dmitry Ternovoy; 190/Jeremy Wee; 210/Creative Commons Zero – creativecommonsstockphotos.

Author's own: 199, 213; 216.